W9-AQK-138

WHAT TO DO
BEFORE & AFTER
SOMEONE DIES

WHAT TO DO BEFORE & AFTER SOMEONE DIES

A practical guide to help you through the
worst possible time for making important decisions

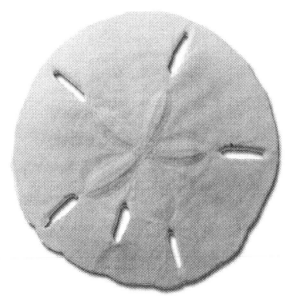

JUDITH LEE

Santa Barbara, California

First Edition
Notice of Rights: All rights reserved. No part of this book may be reproduced or transmitted in any form or by any means, electronic, mechanical, photocopying, recording, or otherwise, without the prior written permission of the publisher.

This publication is designed to educate and provide general information regarding the subject matter covered. It is not intended to replace the counsel of other professional advisors. The reader is encouraged to consult with his or her own advisors regarding specific situations. While the author has taken reasonable precautions in the preparation of this book and believes the facts presented within the book are accurate, neither the publisher nor author assumes any responsibility for errors or omissions. The author and publisher specifically disclaim any liability resulting from the use or application of the information contained in this book. The information within this book is not intended to serve as emotional or therapeutic advice related to individual situations.

Published by Little Moose Press

510 Castillo, Suite #301
Santa Barbara, CA 93101
805-884-9990 Fax: 805-884-9911
www.littlemoosepress.com

Library of Congress Cataloging-in-Publication Data
Lee, Judith Ellen, 1941-
   What to do before & after someone dies : a practical guide to help you through the worst possible time for making important decisions / by Judith Ellen Lee.
       p. cm.
   Summary: "A resource to assist people in making decisions when a friend or loved one is dying or has just died, it includes: helping or being a caregiver, visiting a dying person, what to do when someone dies, making final arrangements, etiquette, talking with survivors and useful phone numbers"--Provided by publisher.
   Includes bibliographical references and index.
   ISBN-10: 0-9720227-8-3 (trade pbk. : alk. paper)
   ISBN-13: 978-0-9720227-8-1 (trade pbk. : alk. paper)
   1. Terminal care. 2. Palliative treatment. 3. Death. 4. Caregivers. 5. Funeral rites and ceremonies. I. Title.
R726.8.L443 2005
616'.029--dc22   2005031048

Printed in the United States of America on acid-free paper.

Wake and Casualty from THE COLLECTED POEMS OF LANGSTON HUGHES by Langston Hughes, © 1994 by The Estate of Langston Hughes. Used by permission of Alfred A. Knopf, a division of Random House, Inc.

Book design: Dotti Albertine
Book production: Patricia Bacall
Editor: Brookes Nohlgren

Good Night

A quaint old book or two to read.
A merry verse or two to write.
A humble prayer or two to plead.
And then...good night.

A laugh or two at well worn jokes.
A song or two in grief's despite.
A loving cup with friendly folks,
And then...good night.

Little I ask, and I would share
That little with an honest friend.
And blithely my small burdens bear
Unto the end.

I've had my day, nor do I fret,
Now fate turns off my feeble light.
God bless you all who linger yet,
Good night...good night.

— Anonymous

/07

Table of Contents

Someone Has Died or Is Dying. What Do You Say? What Do You Do?

You are visiting a friend with a terminal illness. What do you say to them? To their family?

Someone has died and you are handling the details. The problem is, they did not indicate whether they wanted to be buried or cremated. What are your responsibilities? What are your options?

You are going to a funeral of a friend or co-worker whose faith or culture you are not familiar with. Does it matter what color clothing you wear? Are you supposed to bring a condolence gift?

An ill friend has died in their home. You had said you would take care of the final arrangements. What calls do you make? What do you do with the body? How do you deal with their young child?

A loved one has been cremated. They loved camping in the national park. Can you scatter their ashes there?

You want to write a condolence card. What do you say? What should you be sure not to say?

Judith Lee has researched and addressed all these questions and made their answers available and easily accessible. If you are responsible for the details before or after a death, there are certain things you must do. And some things you must not do. There are decisions to be made that can not be unmade. All too often, these have not been anticipated, so you will make them on the spot and then everyone will have to live with them from then on.

What To Do Before & After Someone Dies will allow you to be prepared. You can know what to do in advance, or you can consult it at every stage of the process. It can show you how to assist someone to prepare for death and it can take you through the steps after the event.

It is a valuable guide you can look through any time, and use at the time you will need it most.

JUDITH LEE holds an MA in Psychology with an emphasis on death and dying and is a veteran of the nursing home industry. She founded the Death & Dying Information Center and has created a number of resources to assist people during the challenging times leading up to and immediately after the death of a loved one. She divides her time between Hawai'i and Los Angeles and enjoys a thriving practice speaking to groups and consulting with individuals on the subject of handling the details of death and dying.

Mahalo to . . .

For a project of this size a great many people helped put this book together. In the Appendix under "References" is a long list of people and organizations. All were very kind and so very helpful. A special "mahalo plenty" to the editorial readers: Ruby Oliver, Maryann Campbell, Barbara Joseph, Jacquie Taylor, Kay Lee, Virginia McLoed, Debbi Glanstein, Andrew L. Snyder and Karin Hilsdale.

The inspiration for this book happened in the office of Sue Bowler-Cortez, who was a social worker for a nursing home. The question we discussed was: "Why do the family and friends of a deceased client in the nursing home don't seem to know what to do?" Karin Hilsdale nurtured the beginnings.

To Ellen Reid, my book shepherd, with me through thick and thin; Dotti Albertine, cover designer extraordinaire; Patricia Bacall, patient layout artist; Roberta Krell, Ph.D., Folklore and Genontology editor; Laren Bright, copywriter, whose words for me are magic; Bob Hankins, photographer . . . you are pretty darn good with that digital camera; and Jack Barnard, media coach . . . everyone in this biz needs someone like you . . . heck, they need you!

Thanks mom. Noché. Noché.

DISCLAIMER

This book is designed to provide information in regard to the subject matter covered. It is sold with the understanding that the publisher and author are not engaged in rendering legal, accounting, therapy or other professional services. If legal or other expert assistance is required, the services of a competent professional should be sought.

It is not the purpose of this book to reprint all the information that is otherwise available to the author and/or publisher, but to complement, amplify and supplement other texts. You are urged to read all the available material, learn as much as possible about death and dying and how it relates to you and your situation.

Every effort has been made to make this book as complete and as accurate as possible. However, there may be mistakes both typographical and in content. Therefore, this text should be used only as a general guide and not as the ultimate source of death related information. Furthermore, this book contains information on death and dying only up to the printing date.

The purpose of this book is to educate and entertain. The author and the publisher shall have neither liability nor responsibility to any person or entity with respect to any loss or damage caused, or alleged to be caused, directly or indirectly by the information contained in this book.

If you do not wish to be bound by the above, you may return this book to the publisher for a full refund.

How To Use This Book

*"There is no cure for birth or death
save to enjoy the interlude."*

— George Santayana, author

It was early evening. Sue and David were driving on a divided highway towards Atlantic City, New Jersey. Because of the chilly late fall air the car windows were shut and the radio was playing. Coming out of a curve they saw a car across the divider had flipped; the wheels were still spinning and the headlights of the flipped car were the only illumination. They stopped and ran to the eerily quiet car. There was a heavy odor of gasoline. They first spotted a young man, his upper torso flung through the driver's door window, face down. With little room between the car and the tarmac of the road David crawled to the young man, sought a pulse and looked at his face. The young man was dead. It was then the wail that turned into a shriek began. It came from the back seat area.

There was very little space between the blacktop and the car frame, less than window size. David was too big, but Sue managed to squeeze her head and shoulders inside the back seat window. A teenage girl was wedged on the up-side-down roof of the car, hurt and scared. Wailing, she cried for her mama. David dashed back to his car to call for help. The car phone wasn't working. He waited for another car to come along, worried the flipped car would explode.

Up until this time Sue had never seen a person die but she thought the young girl might be badly hurt and possibly dying. While scared of the gas fumes and possible explosion, she couldn't leave this young girl alone in the dark. Sue put her arms around the girl and spoke softly to calm her down. In the pitch black they couldn't see one another.

The young girl died in Sue's arms.

Few people are introduced to death in such a dramatic way. In fact, few people are even introduced to death. Less than 20% of the United States' population has had a personal experience with the death of someone. It is possible to go through life without ever being with a dying person or seeing death in person. Countless polls have shown that people want to die at home, yet over 80% die in a facility, usually alone or with an employee of the facility. There is more public violence that is producing deaths suddenly and traumatically. Today in the United States 6,000 people a day die and 90% of the people responsible for the deceased have no idea what to do. America is a nation of people who have little experience with death and the dying, and very few have any idea of what needs to be done.

What about the living, those who visit with someone who is dying? How many know what to do or say to a dying person. Whether this person is a stranger, loved one, or friend dying on the street, at home or in a facility, how does one offer support or help?

A loved one dies. What is to be done next? A stranger dies and you are there. What to do? When someone dies what is the first thing that needs to be done by the survivors? What does one do if someone dies in a medical facility? At home? Out of the country? On the street? How many know what is available for the disposition of human remains?

In our multicultural society, how many people are invited to a funeral or want to offer condolences to people of another culture or religion? What does one need to know in order not to embarrass oneself or offend others? Out of the fear of appearing insensitive many people are afraid of coming into contact with the dying, the dead and their survivors. This fear can stem from not knowing what to do or say, or from deeply held cultural beliefs.

Of the material available to the public, how much is easily accessible and understandable? In addition to traditional information what are the current trends? What are the new ways of accessing information?

People learn from experience — the experience of learning what to do when someone dies. Seeking information while upset, grief stricken or confused can lead to misunderstandings, bad judgments and further confusion. Decisions must be made within minutes, hours or days. This emotional maelstrom is added to the dearth of information and the profusion of misinformation.

This book sorts out things as simply as possible. The reader may peruse the entire book, enjoying the real life anecdotes and interesting quotes with the information presented in a clear, easy-to-read style. This will give a good overview of what one needs to know about death itself or if one is responsible for a person who is dying. This book can be used for individuals who wish to plan ahead for themselves as well.

This book can also be used as a reference book. The book is divided into topics and chapters kept as short and simple as possible. All sub-headings are numbered and listed in the Table of Contents. There is an Index at the end of the book for looking up specific words. There is an extensive Appendix with useful resources.

The subject of death is huge and complex... and scary or mysterious to many. This book, the first in a series, helps to simplify and demystify life's most final act without lessening the sacredness of death itself and the emotions of those left behind.

◆

"When I am too old and feeble to follow my sheep or cultivate my corn, I plan to sit in the house, carve Katcina dolls, and tell my nephews and nieces the story of my life...

Then I want to be buried in the Hopi way. Perhaps my boy will dress me in the costume of a Special Officer, place a few beads around my neck, put a paho and some sacred corn meal in my hand, and fasten inlaid turquoise to my ears. If he wishes to put me in a coffin, he may even do that, but he must leave the lid unlocked, place food near by, and set up a grave ladder so that I can climb out. I shall hasten to my dear ones, but I will return with good rains and dance as a Katcina in the plaza with my ancestors..."

— Don Talayesva (late 19th century)
Hopi Sun Clan chief
Native American Wisdom

PART I
BEING WITH
A DYING PERSON

"It is always so hard to let go...
The difficulty of deciding
is compounded by the difficulty
of living with what has been decided."

— Sherwin Nuland, M.D.
author, *How We Die*

It's Not Easy

"He and I could never talk about death."

— Rachel Robinson,
widow of baseball great,
Jackie Robinson

Joseph was dying. He wasn't old, only 43, and he was in denial about his impending death. He had heard whispers about long-ago European Jewish relatives dying in camps during the World War II Holocaust. Indeed, he had been named for his grandfather, who had died in one of the camps. His mother and father, with him at the hospital, were bewildered by the fact that their son seemed to totally ignore the reality of his situation. He didn't speak of the future with his wife, kids and parents. He owned his business and it was left in limbo. His family was frantic as well as grief stricken. His family didn't know what to do or say to Joseph.

They arranged for his grandmother, who had survived the camps and had been one of the family's earliest immigrants to the United States, to fly in for a visit. Very old but in good health, she shooed the family out of Joseph's hospital room and settled in for a long visit. The two of them had been close when Joe was growing up. Like many American families, the young had scattered, but she knew her grandson and they talked.

Upon leaving Joseph's room the family gathered around the old woman. She told them Joseph wanted to talk with them. During the next couple of days Joseph was able to talk about his impending death to his wife and business partner about the future without him.

The family was amazed. What had happened during the grandmother's visit? The grandmother knew her grandchild and the family history. While visiting with Joseph she realized he, quite unconsciously, felt a responsibility to his family, to his grandmother, as the namesake of his long deceased grandfather he had never met. Death was looked at as a failure to fulfill that obligation.

Holding his hand, Jospeh's grandmother chatted about Joseph's niece who had recently become pregnant with her first child. The great joy had been tempered by the sorrow of his illness. When possible complications in the pregnancy had dictated various tests to be done and the gender of the fetus was known, none of this had been told to Joseph, who, by then, was in the hospital. His grandmother told him of the various tests that had been done, how everything looked good and that the babe was to be a boy. That boy was to be named Joseph after his Uncle Joseph in a long time Jewish tradition, wherein members of the family are often named after deceased loved ones.

For Joe this brought comfort and eased his guilt. The name would continue in the family. He died two weeks later at peace with himself. His family was able to say good-bye and take care of personal and business decisions.

This true story illustrates the stress and fear from both a dying person and those around him. That stress and fear can bring miscommunication or even no communication. The dying person, the caregiver(s), the people around them, and the visitors are interacting with one another. One needs to understand what is happening physically, mentally and emotionally to all concerned. The chapters in *Part I: Being With A Dying Person*, will explore the physical process of dying, the psychological concerns of the dying and those around them, the role of the caregiver, suggestions for the visitor, and suggestions for visiting the dying when children are involved.

The Dying Process

"The size of the heart, in the adult, measures
five inches in length, three inches and a half
in breadth in the broadest part, and two inches
and a half in thickness..."

— Gray's Anatomy, 1901

A person may die from something acutely traumatic such as a heart attack or gunshot, or an illness such as liver cancer. The dying process may be different for trauma or illness. For example, a heart attack could possibly produce difficulty in breathing and moderate-to-severe pain and discomfort. On the other hand, a disease such as liver cancer could produce terrible pain that increases over time. People's bodies react differently, so it is hard to pinpoint exact characteristics.

As a caregiver or visitor, people have some trepidation of being with a dying person since they don't know how the person will look or behave. This fear can mean the dying have fewer visitors and fewer people to care for them. If one has some knowledge of what can be happening with the patient there is less fear of the unknown.

Here are some of the physical things that may happen in the dying process with some basic differences between trauma and illness:

2.1 Coma

A coma may happen two different ways. A trauma to the body, such as a car accident, can cause a coma that may last for years.

If the coma is from illness a person may be "slipping into a coma," which is part of the dying process itself. What that means is that the person slowly loses consciousness, becomes unable to speak, and non-responsive. The person may or may not open his or her eyes. Perhaps there will be some kind of response such as being able to squeeze someone's hand or blink the eyes.

Many times, of the five senses, the ability to hear may be the last sense to go. So even if the person is in a coma or coma-like state, continue speaking because hearing may remain intact.

2.2 Breathing

The mouth may be open with a wheezing-type breathing. This is sometimes referred to as the "death rattle." Breathing becomes slower and shallow, and there are longer and longer pauses between breaths.

2.3 Losing Control of Bodily Functions

A visitor may see a tube that goes from the patient's bladder to a bag on the side of the bed to collect urine. This is a good way to keep a person's skin clean and dry and to prevent skin irritation. Incontinent patients may have extra padding under their bottoms or diapers, being changed as needed.

Congestion in the lungs or the back of the throat and inability to swallow or cough could necessitate the nurse/care-giver putting a tube down the throat and/or back of the mouth for a suction machine to remove thick phlegm and permit drainage in the nose and mouth.

If the patient is unable to move, the caregiver would periodically turn (from back to side to stomach to side, as an example) the person. Also, giving the patient a backrub or massage is a comfort measure. Doing these two things prevents the skin from breaking down due to being in the same position for a long period.

2.4 Pain

Groaning, rapid breathing pattern, and grimacing are ways the body may be reacting to pain. Arms, legs and hands may twitch due to involuntary muscle spasms and pain.

2.5 Possible Medicinal Interventions:

Hydration - If a person can't drink or swallow a tube can be placed into a vein with glucose (sugar) or saline solution (salt water) for maintaining body fluids. This is considered a "comfort measure", not a feeding tube, and can prolong life.

Feeding - Patients may have a feeding tube that goes through their nose or mouth into their stomach through which liquid nutrition is provided. This may be their treatment in the disease process since they are unable to eat or drink. During the dying process, depending on their wishes, or the authorized agent's wishes (the person legally responsible), this treatment may be discontinued.

Pain Management - This may be done by several different methods. By injection; a duragesic patch (looks like a small 2-by-3 inch square patch of saran wrap) that is time-released and is changed every few days; a tube going into a vein with pain medicine at a slow constant flow which is called a "drip." There are also rectal suppositories.

Additional Types of Care - The patient may be hooked to various machines such as a heat monitor, sleep apnea or oxygen. A common problem for patients is bed sores. The skin breaks down where it is in constant contact with the bed. The patient needs to be moved and bandaging done to the affected areas.

2.6 How a Person May Look While on Pain Medication

The patient may be sleepy, slow to respond. If starting into the coma process, pain medication may speed up that process.

The breathing may become slowed. May look like the person is not breathing because of long pauses between breaths.

There may be some involuntary twitching of the body that doesn't necessarily mean the person is in more pain but could perhaps be the effect of the pain medication on the nervous system.

As the dying process continues the person may have more pain and need more pain medication. If someone is using pain medication for some time, their body may build up a tolerance requiring increased dosages to control pain. The idea of the dying becoming addicted to their pain relief medication has been proven to be a myth, but continues to be a concern for medical personnel, patients and loved ones.

2.7 Near Death

There may be some body stiffness. The skin color and nails may be pale, gray or bluish because the circulation of blood is slowing. With a dark-skinned person the color change can be noticed around the nails, lips and under the eyelid.

2.8 At the Time of Death

The sound of the lungs collapsing, known as the "death rattle" may or may not happen, but can be startling to hear. Breathing will stop; the chest won't rise anymore. The heart will stop and the skin can become increasingly pale or blue. The chin has a certain slackness upon death.

2.9 How a Person Looks at the Time of Death

Illness — *long-term, cumulative process.* Perhaps excessive weight loss, arms and legs begin stiffening, eyes may be open with eyeballs rolled back, and mouth may be open. Skin color changes from pale to blue and the body becomes cold to the touch. The muscles that control urination and the bowel relax with the urine and bowel contents expelled. It is possible, due to the illness, the deceased will not expel a great deal of urine and bowel content as there was little being digested.

Trauma — *short-term, immediate process.* An example is an auto accident. The body may appear healthy, the eyes may be open, the eyeballs rolled back, and the mouth may be open or closed. The stiffening of the body, skin color change and temperature drop may be slower to start and proceed than from illness because the person was healthy to begin with. If the person has eaten/drunk within several hours, the urine and bowel contents will be expelled.

The Psychological Process

"Death must simply become the discreet but dignified
exit of a peaceful person from a helpful society that is
not torn, not even overly upset by the idea of a
biological transition without significance, without pain
or suffering, and ultimately without fear."

— Philippe Ariès, author,
The Hour Of Our Death

For the most part, a dying person's physical problems, as outlined in the previous chapter, are fairly easy to see, feel or hear. The psychological process is less easy to see. Therefore it is important that the caregivers and visitors around the dying person have some understanding of not only what is happening psychologically with the patient, but with other participants also. Denial, anger, lethargy and mourning can be felt by all involved in the dying process.

The type of death can further complicate this. Is it unexpected? Expected? Has this been a long time in coming? The type of death, be it from a disease or trauma like murder, has a psychological impact on not only the victim but also those around him/her.

There is a relationship between the dying person and those around that person. Discomfort, guilt, anger and conflict may be present. Close loved ones of a dying person may feel emotionally one way while relative strangers may feel another. When children are involved, whether they be the one dying or the offspring of the dying, another dimension is added to the psychological process.

Unlike the physical process, with a straightforward listing of physical characteristics, the psychological dynamics are much more complex. This chapter will attempt to give the reader a basic sense of what one could be experiencing.

3.1 Becoming Critically/Deathly Ill

Elisabeth Kübler-Ross, a psychiatrist and best-selling author during the 1970s on death and dying, identified five stages a person facing death (and other trauma) may go through. Over the past two or three decades there has been debate amongst grief therapists on these stages and if they should even be called "stages". However, they do help people understand what is happening with a critically ill or dying person.

There is no set length of time a critically ill or dying person will embrace any of the stages, nor will any given person pass through them in any particular order, or even "complete" all the stages. The thing to remember is that the dying person can be going through any of these feelings: denial, rage and anger, bargaining, depression, or acceptance.

3.2 Kübler-Ross Five Stages

1. **Denial: "No, not me."**
   This is a typical reaction when a person learns that he or she is terminally ill.
2. **Rage and anger: "Why me?"**
   The person resents the fact that others will remain healthy and alive while he or she must die.
3. **Bargaining: "Yes me, but..."**
   Person accepts the fact of death but strikes bargains for more time.
4. **Depression.**
   First, the person mourns past losses, things not done, wrongs committed. But then he/she enters a state of "preparatory grief," getting ready for the arrival of death.
5. **Acceptance: "My time is very close now and it's all right."**

3.3 The Psychological Dynamics

The five stages listed require that the dying person have the time to go through all of these stages. What happens if death is a result of instant trauma, such as a gunshot or auto accident? Does the dying person in this situation go through the stages? Again, this is not something that happens to all who are dying, but it can happen that the dying go through these thoughts or feelings in minutes, if not seconds. To a visitor, a caregiver or even a relative stranger it is valuable information to realize the dying person can be going through some of these listed feelings in any situation.

A person who is dying can be embarrassed by the situation and they may wish to be left alone. In the United States it is common to consider one is "at war" with terminal illness. Because of difficult breathing or pain or various machines hooked up to their bodies, some people may feel less than human, with shame at "losing the war" with the disease/trauma and losing control.

The Kübler-Ross five stages are a guideline for all parties concerned. While originally written with the dying person in mind, it has been found that people who know the dying person, or even think they know the person, can go through a form of the five stages. Think of a loved one who was in your life. When you found out that person was dying there could have been denial, anger or depression. Your anger could have been directed towards the dying ("How dare you die!"), or towards the fate that has brought this death ("How dare my loved one die!").

These stages can be seen in people who experience a loss of someone they only think they know, such as the death of famous people. When Princess Diana was killed in an auto accident, it was completely unexpected, and with the first words of the news hitting the public, there was denial.

"No, it couldn't be her! Our Princess? No!" The public couldn't take the news in and accept it. Except for family and friends, nobody really knew the Princess, but at the time of her death millions of people felt some kind of kinship and went through some of the five stages.

A List Of Legal And
Medical Terms to Know

"The big 'D'..., I never think of it."

— Henry Mancini, composer,
shortly before he died

4.1 The Will

Do you have a will or a trust? Have you made your wishes known as to what you want done with your body after your death? What kind of funeral do you want? These are some of the questions that are answered with a will or trust. While a will doesn't necessarily need to be drawn up by an attorney, a trust does, as it is more complicated. If you have minor children a will can be used to allow the children to be cared for by whomever you have named as their guardian. If you have assets such as property, investments or cash in accounts, the government will only allow your wishes as to dispersion through a will or trust. And oftentimes, even if you just have "family treasures" there can be a fight among your survivors, unless you have designated who gets what. Naming the person who will be responsible for your body after death and what kind of funeral you want can be done through a will or trust. Without a will or trust the state may name an administrator to deal with the estate left by the deceased.

4.2 Power of Attorney

Giving a person a durable power of attorney for you means that person is allowed to handle your affairs. Examples are specific transactions, running your business or making legal decisions. A power of attorney is generally not recognized by financial institutions and becomes invalid when the person who named the power of attorney dies.

A durable power of attorney is almost always drafted so people can handle another person's affairs when very ill, dying, hospitalized, senile or otherwise incompetent. As an example, a person could be dying and would like to sell his car as he can't drive any longer. The selling of the car can involve trips, paperwork and seeing of people, all things the dying person isn't able to do. Someone with durable power of attorney for the dying person would be able to sell the car on his or her behalf.

There are advantages and disadvantages in using a power of attorney, so make sure advice and counsel is sought from a lawyer or someone who is an expert in this area.

4.3 The Medical Directive

A medical directive is a document in which competent people try to contemplate what medical interventions they would want or not want should they lose mental/physical capacity in the future. The directive may also include the naming of "Durable Power of Attorney for Health Care" and list their responsibilities. It can include an ombudsman witness (if entering a facility) and other such documents as a "Do Not Resuscitate" form. It is generally regarded as the preferred legal document, unlike the older version, which was called a "Living Will."

What this means is that people are now allowed to decide what kind of medical treatment they would want to be given or withheld at the end of life. A dying person has a wide array of medical treatment to choose from. Some people want everything the medical profession can offer to keep them alive. Others want nothing and some want something in between. This is something one would want to think about and discuss with doctors, caregiver, loved ones and close friends. Once healthcare decisions are made this information is placed in the document. Copies of this document are given to your doctor or clinic, your power of attorney person, treating facility and homecare agency. Health organizations, hospitals, the Internet, health associations and health-related government departments will have Medical Directive packets. You should not have to pay for a Medical Directive form.

4.4 Durable Power of Attorney for Health Care

A competent person formally designates someone to make medical/health decisions should the competent person lose the capacity to make such decisions. This form is usually found in the Medical Directive packet. It involves naming a person and having witnesses or a notary sign and spell out what the person named can or cannot do. Unless specified the DPAHC responsibilities become invalid upon the dying person's death. If the DPAHC is to be the authorized agent for body disposition and/or funeral arrangements, these wishes must be listed.

4.5 The "Do Not Resuscitate" Form

This is a decision made by the dying person of sound mind, or the authorized agent if the dying person is not competent. When a person has an unexpected life-threatening problem and he or she is at home or out in public, 911 is called, paramedics respond and resuscitate the person. Their job is to give people emergency medical care, stabilize them and transport them to the hospital. If this problem happens in the hospital, medical personnel are summoned immediately and they too, are there to keep people alive and stabilized enough to decide on further medical treatment.

Individuals or authorized agents may decide they do not want resuscitation and have a right to have this wish recognized. This often is the case when a person has a terminal illness, incapacitating illness or trauma and resuscitation is considered simply invasive and not wanted. An example is someone who has had multiple strokes or heart attacks within a short span of time and is brought "back to life" with resuscitation each time. That individual may decide not to have any more resuscitation. One makes this wish known by filling out the "Do Not Resuscitate" form.

As awareness of this right is becoming better known, this form is popping up in more places. More and more hospitals and nursing facilities have the form available for patients as part of the paper-work. The patient or authorized agent can always request the form if not offered. Medical staff or doctors and nurses, may not know if their hospital has one and you may have to seek out an office clerk to actually get the form.

If one wishes to have this completed form as part of their Medical Directive, make sure the Medical Directive has the form, or pick one up at a local hospital, nursing facility or online. Various organizations are offering this form as part of a Patient's Rights packet.

If the patient is receiving home care or hospice care, these agencies must be aware of the DNR form. You may want to put the form in an easily accessible place such as hanging on the refrigerator, bulletin board, or at the head of the bed itself.

4.6 Authorized Agent

In death there is a hierarchy for who is responsible for the deceased. It is spouse, (adult) offspring, parents, siblings, other biological family members, and lastly, non-family. Technically speaking, if there is no biological family member responsible, a non-family member must have an "authorized agent" form signed by the deceased (obviously prior to their death) giving the person named the right to be responsible for the body of the deceased upon their death. Even biological family members may need to produce authorization upon demand.

Being the "authorized agent" is different from having "power of attorney" and "durable power of attorney for health care" (DPAHC). Those two are only during the life of the ill or dying person. Upon death they are not valid unless it specifically states that person is responsible for the disposition of the body and funeral arrangements. Quite often the same person who has "power of attorney" and/or "durable power of attorney for health care" for the ailing/dying person may be the same person who is responsible for disposition of the body and funeral arrangements as they are the "authorized agent" for the deceased.

If an individual enters into a health care facility, the naming of the person responsible for the individual upon their death will be part of the paperwork completed upon admission. If the individual wishes to fill out the form prior to actually needing it, then the individuals must take it upon themselves to procure and fill out the form. These forms may be found at Health Maintenance Organizations (HMO's), some doctors' offices (ask the office personnel), local health departments, and the Internet. Some hospitals have generic forms.

Realistically, it is often a non-biological family member who ends up responsible for the deceased. Vivien, 78, and Harry, 84, while living in different states, were a "part-time couple." She visited him and he visited her. When Harry died it was Vivien who called the funeral home, made the arrangements, paid for everything, received Harry's cremated remains, made the trip to his apartment to sort and take his few possessions, and contacted both his immediate and extended family, with whom he had not been close.

Neither the Veteran's Hospital or funeral home asked her for an "authorized agent" form, nor did his family question her. Harry was poor, his death wasn't traumatic or unusual and the funeral arrangements were simple. If the deceased is wealthy, or if death is traumatic or questionable this can complicate the situation. An "authorized agent" form/card may be needed at a coroner's office, emergency room in a hospital, police, government offices or funeral home. Both legal and financial organizations can require this form.

If two people live together without a legal marriage it is very important that each make the other an "authorized agent" if they wish to have that person responsible for their body disposition and funeral arrangements. George and Martin, partners for 27 years, for example, never thought to have "authorizing agents" drawn up. When Martin died, his sister, who had not been close to Martin for many years, had Martin's body flown many miles away and held a funeral to which George was not invited.

The Caregiver

*"Some days, even the most devoted caregiver
wishes their Alzheimer's victim dead. Their spirits
are lifted by the caring members of support groups
and Hale Kako'o (H'awaiian meaning: a place to aid,
support, uphold and bind together) Respite Center
allows them time off."*

— Iz Campbell, caregiver and board member,
Alzheimer's Association, Honolulu Chapter, Inc.

On any given day there are approximately 25 million people caring for someone who has a terminal or ongoing illness. This can be a twenty-four hours a day, seven days a week job. Most caregivers are family members of the ill person; however, not all family members can or want to be caregivers. This can add to the stress of the person who is the caregiver. Professional caregivers who work or volunteer in a facility or come to the ill person's home are able to "leave the job" on a daily basis, although they, too, can invest feelings and emotion toward their patients.

Caregivers should understand that having the feelings that Iz Campbell expresses are very normal. In fact, it would be rather abnormal if a caregiver didn't have such thoughts. Often the caregivers will feel a sense of relief upon the death of the ill person. And why not? It is a relief. The physical work can be exhausting and never ending. The emotional toll can be devastating. Guilt, while common, is not warranted.

Expressed in the quote above is the importance of support and help. Whether it is a center such as Hale Kako'o in Hawai'i or friends and family giving the caregiver a much needed break, it is valuable for both the patient and the caregiver. Caregiving is a stressful job and burnout can happen quickly. Long-term dying, whether it be from a terminal illness, trauma or a slow deterioration of both physical and mental faculties, (such as Alzheimer's), is hard on all involved.

Family and friend caregivers, for the most part, do not get to volunteer for the job or get training. A new profession, training non-professional caregivers, is being started by people who have been caregivers themselves.

5.1 Traditional Caregivers — Family and Professional

Close to 80% of caregivers are women, and the majority take care of the sick at home. For the very wealthy, or those opting for extended care insurance, there can be full-time professional caregivers, but for the average family it is a family member who assumes this role, providing care on a daily basis, 24 hours a day. Depending on financial resources the caregiver may have part-time professional help such as a nurse or an aide.

Nursing homes provide professional caregivers, but many times, a family member or friend will still visit on a regular basis, both as a comfort for the ill patient and to assure that nursing home is providing good care. It is not unusual to see a family member or friend with a patient helping with care-giving chores such as bathing, feeding or changing the patient's clothes.

Hospice, which is care for the dying, may be much like a nursing home with full-time professional care, or it may be a home-hospice with trained volunteers and professionals coming to the home. These professionals could include nurses, social workers, aides and religious personnel. Hospice services can be provided in a nursing home. Again, depending on the financial resources of the family and/or the insurance benefits, aides may be part of the hospice package. But for the majority of people, even with hospice at home, it is a family member, usually a woman, who will be the primary caregiver.

5.2 A New Trend: The Fragmented Family

Millions more Americans are facing their illness and/or impending death alone, far from family or with no family at all. Between 1970 and 1990 the percentage of single or divorced adults in America rose from 19.4% to 30.5%. During the same time period the proportion of Americans living alone jumped from 8% to 13%, totalling 23 million people. The traditional caregiver, the family, is disappearing. Sometimes stepping into this void are friends who are acting as caregivers and confidantes.

Lydia had cancer that was spreading, and her energy level was dropping quickly. With no family, some of her friends who had visited her became her caregivers. They all had busy lives of their own, as well as individual talents and tolerance for their friend's illness. One friend who did not work for a living became the "coordinator" and made sure errands, bill paying and social visits were done in a timely fashion.

When Lydia decided she wanted to arrange for what would be done with her body after her death she was shy about talking to her friends. Her "coordinator" friend found out and together they picked a friend who could help Lydia.

Whether the caregiver is a family member or friend, their role is vital. The ill person needs care and it is the caregiver who tends to their needs and makes constant decisions, trying to provide not only physical care but emotional and perhaps even spiritual care as well. The caregiver will usually be the one to decide if the sick person can have visitors. This is a tremendous job and many people are not prepared to become a caregiver.

5.3 Four Things the Caregiver Must Think About

Talking about death. Americans often find it distasteful, overwhelming or frightening to talk about death or disability. Few families sit down and talk about one's future death or possible disability. Therefore it just seems to happen. One day a grown child will realize his or her parent(s) are too frail or sickly to be independent or that a loved one/friend is dying and will need care. The dying people themselves often are in denial and can't talk about their impending death.

The "in-between" generation. This is the generation who has responsibility for elderly or sick parents or loved ones, for their own children and, quite often, a career. This generation is called upon to care for many people in many different places. The role of caregiver for the dying is generally a full-time effort; therefore, if a caregiver-to-be has family and job responsibilities at the same time, the realization can be devastating to all concerned.

Fragmentation of the family unit. Family members are physically living apart, often at great distances. Due to financial constraints or responsibilities it may be very hard, even impossible to become a caregiver.

How does the caregiver-to-be feel about death? Can the individual handle the dying process? If the caregiver has difficulty with death, dying, or the patient's wishes, the stressful situation can become intolerable. If the caregiver is feeling resentful of the burden, the care often will be less than needed. Resentment can lead to anger. If the caregiver is in denial while the patient is at another stage psychologically, their relationship will be very stressful.

5.4 Three Topics to be Discussed by the Patient and the Caregiver

The Environment. There are a many things to think about when one wishes to die at home. It needs to be comfortable for the dying person, the caregiver and the survivors. If a lot of medical intervention is needed or wanted, would home be the best place? Don't feel pressured or guilty about moving the dying loved one to a medical facility. If the dying person is mentally competent, then there can be a discussion with the family/ authorized agent. If the dying person is mentally incompetent, the decision will rest with the family or authorized agent.

If the situation is such that the dying person will be at a medical facility, has this been discussed between the dying person and the person or people responsible for the patient? There can be guilt on the part of the caregiver if the patient has to be moved to a facility. This can result in the caregiver not wanting to discuss the pending move with the patient. The patient may not want to be moved and would find it hard to discuss this as well.

Relationship between the caregiver and patient. Is this a mutually loving or at least likable relationship? Does one have a superior or dominating role to the other? How might that role be changed as the patient becomes sicker? Are others involved? Are they bringing their own agendas or opinions to the situation?

Caregiver's issues, as discussed earlier in this chapter. Many people find themselves caregivers without being able to plan for the situation. The individual may have issues of fear or revulsion toward death or dying, or feel resentment at having to be a caregiver. A very private person now needs to interact with other people who will be visiting, or someone with no decision-making skills now find themselves needing to make decisions constantly.

A dying patient who is fully cognizant may eventually lose some or all of their mental capability because of their illness. Elderly people can be afflicted with senile dementia and be unable to participate in their own care. The caregiver and patient need to talk over the issues raised here before the patient is no longer able to have these discussions. However, in any circumstance, all people can use care, compassion and loving kindness.

The Visitor

"Oh, I am so bored with it all."

— Sir Winston Churchill, British Prime Minister,
last words before dying

Quite often when a person is very ill or dying, people around them may seem to disappear. People experiencing these disappearances have called it the "ghost syndrome" and attribute it to a number of causes. It may be a way for a person to "prepare" for the upcoming grief of the loss. It also can be because of the fear of one's own mortality. And it can be that the people around the dying person are so uncomfortable in this particular social setting that they don't know what to say or do. Therefore visitors may stay away. There are other visitors who think nothing of barging in and ignoring the wishes of the dying or the caregiver. This, too, is done out of ignorance. Let's see if we can't sort out this most delicate of social occasions.

Unless you are the caregiver for someone who is dying, the usual way for a person to find out someone is very ill or dying is from a phone call. Someone will call you or you will run into a friend who will tell you of the illness. Occasionally one will see a newspaper article. However you obtain the information, the idea of visiting a dying person may make you nervous. A lot of that nervousness can be due to not knowing what will happen when you visit, or how the dying person will appear.

6.1 Basic List of Questions to Ask Before the First Visit

Whether one is going to visit in a private home or a medical facility, there are some questions to ask ahead of time. A quick phone call before the visit will help the visitor, the caregiver and the dying person. If the visit is to a private home the call would be to the caregiver. If the visit is to a medical facility the questions may be asked of the person or people responsible for the patient (perhaps a family member or friend), or at the nurses' station.

1. Does the dying person know that he or she is dying? This can be a sensitive situation. Caregivers, rightly or wrongly, may have the responsibility of informing the dying person that he or she is, in fact, dying. This situation often depends on the personalities of the people involved. Medical personnel, doctors and nurses, as well as familial caregivers may decide the dying individual doesn't need to know. The dying person may, in fact, not want to know.

You may or may not agree with this reasoning, so what do you do? When you ask the caregiver how informed the dying person is, notice how and what the caregiver answers. The caregiver could be in denial or is doing what he or she "thinks best" for the dying person. Doctors may or may not inform patients they are dying and leave that to family members.

As a visitor do you have the right to tell the caregiver they must inform the dying person of their condition? Do you have the right to tell the dying person? This is one of life's dicey moments and there is no absolute "yes" or "no" answer.

Don't say anything until you have visited with the dying person. One's own death, when you think about it, is a very intimate thing, and it is quite possible that one visit is not enough time in your relationship with a dying person to discuss this.

2. Do the people around the dying person know the patient is dying? Sometimes the dying person *does* know that he or she is dying even though the people around that person do not discuss it, or do not know.

John was dying from complications due to AIDS. His mom flew into town and was with him every day. She did not know he had AIDS. He was afraid to tell her as he thought he would be giving her further anguish. After a few days his mother knew something was wrong but couldn't put her finger on it. John was encouraged by another friend to tell her. He did. John and his mother spent his last days together grieving over his impending death. John still didn't want to die, and his mother still had terrible mourning to do, but they shared his last days together.

John's friend was correct, in this instance, in talking it over with John rather than telling John's mother directly. The friend decided it was not her place to tell John's mother of John's AIDS condition. But she also recognized that John, in addition to grieving for his impending death, was also stressed about thinking he had to evade and lie to his mother. It was exhausting for him. The situation didn't allow him to openly grieve. The friend also realized that his mom could suffer additional anguish due to her ignorance of the situation.

3.   What is the best time to visit? The timing of your visit is for the benefit of both the dying person and the caregiver(s). If visiting in a private home, most likely the caregiver(s) are family members, loved ones, friends, or possibly professional help. The family members and loved ones are going through their own grieving and stressful time. Call ahead and ask how long the visit should last. In a medical facility the caregivers could be a combination of family, friends and professionals.

4.   What is the best type of gift? Literally the best gift you can give is your visit and taking the time to call and ask these questions first. If you feel you must bring something, ask the caregiver. It is possible you might be thinking of bringing a gift for the family. Ask the person if there is anything you can bring.

Another suggestion would be to wait until after the first visit. During the visit you may learn of something that the dying person or family would appreciate having. If you will be visiting more than once you will get a sense of what is needed or wanted. A gift suggestion would be to offer to help out the caregiver or dying person's family. If you are comfortable visiting the dying person, have a good sense of the situation, and have the time, offer to help the caregiver/family.

5. How is the dying person feeling? This sounds so basic you might forget to ask. It also would be a good time to ask how the caregiver is feeling. This also gives you a chance to "get a feel" for the situation that will help alleviate your nervousness.

6.2 Additional Questions Before a Visit to a Medical Facility

1. What is the name and address of the facility? If the dying person is about to be or has been transferred to a facility (a hospital, nursing home or hospice), make sure you get the full name and the address. Often there are facilities with the same owner and which have similar names. You could end up at the wrong place.

2. What are the visiting hours? Many facilities have certain hours for visiting. You might also want to ask about parking, or public transportation as well if you are not driving.

3. Are there special rules such as age limit, if any, for visitors?

4. Who should you speak with regarding the patient? Speak to a staff person who is responsible for the patient. In a hospital or nursing home, call the nursing station. In a hospice ask the person answering the phone who to speak to about the patient. You are not calling for confidential medical information (they won't tell you anyhow), but you want to know if it is okay to visit the patient. Don't expect to chat since the staff is very busy.

6.3 Helpful Hints When Visiting

- The majority of home caregivers in the United States are family members, usually women. Whether male or female, all need a respite from stressful situations, and caring for a dying person can be stressful, both emotionally and physically. Offer to help run errands for the caregiver and/or care for the dying person for a certain amount of time so the caregiver may have a break. If the dying process is slow, the offer would be greatly appreciated by the caregiver.

- The dying person, if still alert, might enjoy the company of another person as long as the routine is not broken. Changes in the routine can cause distress to both the dying person and the caregiver.
- Don't have just eaten a spicy meal. Bad breath can offend anyone. Not only can it offend a dying person, it can also cause nausea because of medication.
- Don't wear perfume, shaving lotion, or bring flowers with a strong scent. A person's sense of smell can be affected by the medication he or she is taking and the scent of perfume, shaving lotion or a flower can actually make that person feel nauseous.
- When visiting a facility and the patient's door is closed, check first with the nurses' station before entering. The patient could be unwell or is being attended to and needs privacy.
- A general rule is to avoid sitting on a patient's bed without asking permission from the dying person. Doing so can cause worsened pain or discomfort.
- Position yourself so the patient does not have to strain to see you. The turning of the head can be painful so it is important you are in their sight line.
- Don't send/bring "Get well" cards. You may want to send/ bring "Thinking of You" cards.
- Don't lose your sense of humor or expect the dying person to have lost his or hers.
- Other patients (in the facility) or other visitors may not know if the patient is dying or even the nature of the sickness. Therefore do not discuss these topics in the presence of others. Check with the caregiver.
- Don't say, "Don't talk like that." "That sounds so depressing." "You'll be better in no time." That isn't the truth, and these phrases may prevent the dying person from sharing fears or other important feelings.

- Be prepared for wildly fluctuating mood swings. This is not an absolute with all dying people but is a common characteristic.
- Don't impose your religious or spiritual beliefs upon a dying person or on those around the dying person.
- Such things as bringing a meal or taking the ill person out to dinner, being with the ill person after surgery, or during a treatment may be welcome.

It took many years, but the cremated remains of Louis Sloan are finally at rest in a place he loved — The Lamplighter Inn in the state of Washington. Before the arrival of his remains, the Inn staff say lights sometimes mysteriously turned off and on and the pool balls moved on the billiards table when no one was near it.

Since the urn, with his remains, has been atop the fireplace mantle in the restaurant portion of the Inn, the ghost has toned down his act. Recent escapades have included tugging on (bartender) Ms. Smith's skirt and patting restaurant owner Michael on the behind.

"He's happier since we've brought him back," said Ms. Smith.

— American Funeral Director Magazine

Being There In The Last Hours Of Life

"We die only once, no practice."

— Makia Malo,
Hawaiian storyteller

Anyone around a dying person, visitor or caregiver, can be feeling much of the same feelings the dying may be going through such as denial, anger, guilt or resentment. However, at some point, the dying person is at the end of their life with only hours or even minutes left. The caregiver(s) and visitors at that time have to focus on what is happening at that moment because there is no second chance. Death erases second chances.

7.1 Being There List

1. **Trust yourself.** Have the courage to trust yourself and what you wish for the one you love. Your intuition, your open heart, and your own inner guidance will direct you.

2. **Let the one you love know you are not going to give up on him or her.** You are very important. What you have to give at this time is as important as anything the medical profession can give.

3. **Touch and be very near.** Dying is a scary time for people and exaggerates feelings of aloneness and isolation. Touching says, "You are not alone, I am with you." Being close and touching are basic ways of showing people that they are loved, safe and cared for.

4. **Speak directly, simply and lovingly.** Make your words easy to understand and clear. Look into the eyes of the one who is ill, even if closed or if there is unconsciousness, as though the eyes are open. Assume you are heard; there is a good chance you are.

5. **Say the things that need to be said.** Make peace in the relationship: forgiveness, appreciation and understanding of the greater purpose of your life together. Share the specific things you love in the other and what his or her life has meant to you. Be gentle, kind, and understanding. It is important that the one who is dying feels cherished, honored, and knows that his or her life has counted. Reminisce, look at scrapbooks, have photographs around the bed.

6. **Acknowledge the need for silence.** Death is deep beyond our understanding. The person who is dying needs time for quiet introspection. Respect this, as you continue to be there with your loving attention and reassuring nearness.

7. **Bring beauty, warmth, and life to the room.** Cherished music, poetry, paintings, flowers from the garden, a non-scented blossom pinned to the pillow or taped to the railing of the bed, pets (if allowed), children (if allowed), a handmade cover, a lovely scarf of soft material for about the neck, a favorite article of clothing to be worn.

8. **Knowing what to do and what to expect does not mean you are surrendering to death.** In fact, when it isn't so feared, it can make you and the one who is dying stronger.

9. **Tell the dying person, "It is ok to go. I will miss you but I will be ok."** Encourage a letting go of the fearful "holding on." In this there is less pain and stress, and the body can more easily respond to any medicine or oxygen being given. And when death comes, it will come with greater ease and gentle relief.

10. **When the actual moment of death comes, resist the impulse to "do something" or take action.** Know this is a precious, holy time, both for you and the one who has died. Continue to be there with your open heart and your loving presence. You may be able to say things you were not able to say earlier. Once you call the nurse, doctor, police or mortuary it is no longer your private time, so take the opportunity for yourself and your family.

7.2 A Special Note for Victims of Trauma

It can be a murder, an accident or an acute physical trauma such as a heart attack. The dying can have only minutes to live. When this happens there is usually a flurry of people trying to get help and there can be people who do not want to be involved at all. Loved ones of victims will usually stay with the victim, often too emotional themselves to comfort the dying. If you are with a stranger, someone you know slightly, or a loved one, don't withdraw but stay in touch with words and perhaps a simple holding of hands. Tell them you are with them. If they want to speak, let them. If you feel yourself starting to cry let the tears flow. When you think about it, that is a nice "gift" to give the dying — your care and concern. Even a stranger can be moved by a person's death.

A note to the squeamish: some areas in the U.S. have professional cleaning businesses that specialize in the clean-up of a death site. Ask the police or paramedics for a referral. Due to the rise in violence in the U.S., this is a business that is growing very fast.

Children

"Now I lay me down to sleep.
I pray the Lord my soul to keep.
If I should die before I wake,
I pray the Lord my soul to take."

— Children's nursery rhyme

For many of us, the saddest of deaths is when a child dies. The scariest of deaths can be when a child's parent or loved one dies. And the most awkward visit for adults can be with a very ill or dying child. When adults become very ill or have a trauma they often end up in a medical facility. This is even more true with children. Issues of patients' rights have made it possible for dying adults or those responsible for them, to decide whether to die at home or in a facility. With children, unless death is fast and unexpected, they will usually die in a facility, since the adult survivors of the child will want to have any medical intervention provided in the possibility of the staving off the horror of a child's death.

8.1 General Suggestions

- **Tell children what is happening.** The age and the maturity of the child will be the guideline. The adults need to answer all of the children's questions openly and honestly. The actual dying process can be too complicated for a very young child to understand, however they could understand someone being "very sick" and could be visiting that "very sick" person.

- **Let them visit the dying.** During the actual visit an adult may want to be with the visitor for at least the beginning of the visit. When the visiting child is finished with the visit don't expect the child to look or act mournful. They may or may not be mournful and sad, or they may be hiding their sadness.

- **Let them have their time to say good-bye.**
- **Is this the right time for a visit?** The dying process of a child, whether it be from illness or trauma, is undeniably one of the hardest, if not the hardest, experience for adults to endure. This goes against the life cycle; the young are born, the old die. When it is turned around the grief can be insurmountable. Because of this the visitor must be particularly diligent in finding out if visiting the dying child is wanted and appropriate. The child may not want visitors, especially if the visitor is a stranger or the child doesn't like the visitor.

8.2 An Adult Visiting a Child

Little Jenai, two years old, had leukemia. She was very sick and spent five months in the hospital. It was touch and go for 3 1/2 months as to whether she would survive. Her mom and grandmother were at the hospital almost continuously. One day grandma was with Jenai, when she rather wanly mentioned her grandfather.

"I hope he comes soon," she said.
"Why?" asked grandma.
"I like grandpa, he makes me laugh," she said.

Jenai's grandfather is an example of a good adult-child visit. Her grandfather didn't bring any of his issues, fears or anger towards his granddaughter's illness with him when visiting the child. He understood her well enough to know a little laugh would do her good and knew how to make her laugh.

Issues of dealing with death and dying of a child can cause adults not to visit as it is just too painful for the adult. That can lead to the dilemma of the adults "abandoning" the child. Ideally there should be a stable adult for the child that can provide help in this dilemma — helping the child feel not so abandoned if other adults do not visit, and monitoring visiting adults if death and dying issues are lurking. The stable adult can intercede.

Parents and loved ones of a dying child quite often are so grief stricken by the situation they cannot deal with visitors, adult or children. It is best that someone in this grief-stricken group have the assignment to decide whether to give permission for a visitor, adult or child.

8.3 A Child Visiting an Adult

Many adults do not want children visiting the dying. The adults are trying to "protect" the child from death. Even if the dying adult is a loved one, children are not always allowed to visit. And, if visiting is allowed, it can be a fast, superficial visit that can do additional harm to the child, leaving feelings of increased anger, confusion and abandonment.

Therefore, it is important to make sure the child can visit. If the adult is a loved one the child may be dealing with many issues. Chief among them will be the child not understanding why the loved one isn't with them. And the younger the child the less he or she will understand exactly what dying and death means. Talk to the child about the impending first-time visit.

8.4 A Child Visiting Another Child

Should a child be allowed to visit another child who is dying? If the dying child is in a medical facility, as is usually the case, the visit will depend partially on whether the rules allow children to visit. Today many facilities are more flexible, but it is best to check first. It will depend on the wishes of adult guardians of the dying child.

In this society children are generally kept away from real death (movies and television are not real). If a child is allowed to visit, an adult close to the child who is doing the visiting, will need to discuss the idea of visiting and explain what is happening with the dying child.

PART II
WHAT TO DO WHEN SOMEONE DIES

UNTITLED

In heathen tribes, where skulls were thick,
did primal passions rage.
They had a system sure and quick
to cure the blight of age.
When one grew old and youth had fled
and time had sapped his vim,
They simply popped him on the head —
which was the last of him.
But now, in our enlightened age,
we're made of finer stuff,
And so we look with righteous rage
on means so crude and rough.
So when our men and women grow old and gray
and bent and short of breath,
We simply take their jobs away
and let them starve to death.

— Anonymous

Now What?

*"Everybody has got to die, but I have always believed
an exception would be made in my case. Now what?"*

— William Saroyan, writer

Leonard, in his late 30s, a tall dark slender man with a gentle nature, was dying. He and his family, on his doctor's recommendation, had him admitted to a nursing home. He lived for several weeks, growing ever weaker with cancer. The afternoon Leonard died family members were with him as he quietly expired. He was sitting and had been propped up with pillows. Toward the end of his life that was the most comfortable position for Leonard, and that was how he died.

One family member became quite upset as Leonard's mouth fell open. A nurse brought in a scarf-sized piece of white cotton material, slipped the material under Leonard's chin and tied it on top of his head. The ends of the white material looked like rabbit ears. The family sat quietly around the bed. Leonard, who always had a dignified look, even with the rabbit ears looked like he was presiding over the group. Like a tableau the family sat still. Leonard sat still. Four hours later the tableau had not moved.

The nursing home rule was that a body would need to be moved off the premises within four hours. This rule, along with others, was always explained to the patient and the person responsible for the patient. When a patient died the nurses were somewhat flexible with this rule, as they knew it was a time of grief for those present.

After four hours a social worker from the social services department went to Leonard's room and spoke to the family. She explained that soon Leonard's body would have to be moved out of the nursing home. The family asked her what should they do. They had absolutely no idea of what to do, who to call, or what had to be done.

This is a very common occurrence. Leonard's family had never discussed, either amongst themselves or with Leonard, what to do after his death. They hadn't sought information as to what needed to be done or had they a plan for the disposition of the body.

In Leonard's case a social worker was able to give the family the name of a funeral provider and let the family know what information would be needed. This family was lucky they were in a situation that allowed for an informed person to help them start the after-death process.

But death doesn't always happen this way. If death is unexpected or the survivors live a distance away from the deceased, what needs to be done? An unexpected death does not give a survivor a long time to seek information about post-death procedures. And if you were seeking information where would it be available? Would you know where to look? What to ask?

People may die at home or in a facility surrounded by loved ones. Death may be unexpected and in a public place, far away from home, or in a foreign country. Whether a person dies unexpectedly, at home, in a medical facility or in a public place, each situation has basic procedures. Those procedures for each situation are covered in this section.

About six days before Ralph Glanstein's death, he asked for Chocolate Kisses. He wanted the taste of chocolate when he died. His family got them for him the day he asked. He died with the taste of chocolate in his mouth.

At The Time Of Death

"That was a great game of golf, fellers."

— Bing Crosby, movie star/singer,
on his deathbed

Death comes in all forms. It can be such that the person literally just quietly expires. There will be no great physical change in the person. Another death can be slow and tortuous, the dying resisting until the end and death comes loudly. And the violent death — a car accident or shooting victim can be very gruesome. For those who are with a loved one or friend at the time of their death this may be the best time for a last good bye with the deceased before the post-death procedures begin.

Grandma Phyllis, age 92, died at home with her son, his wife and kids with her. Within minutes of her death neighbors stopped by to pay their respects to grandma and see how the family was doing. The family had no idea or plans about what to do after grandma died. A niece who had been there while grandma died called a crematorium to arrange the pick up of the body, basic documentation and cremation (after ascertaining from the family that was what they wanted). The family was on a tight budget so the niece called around for the best price.

There were a lot of details and information that needed gathering in the middle of the night. The niece was able to handle the details but she also wanted the family to be able to say goodbye to Phyllis as all had been close to her. The niece gathered the family members together around Phyllis and told them that if anyone wanted private time with Phyllis or to say goodbye this was the time.

The teenage kids, with help of friends who had also been there during Phyllis's death scoured the neighborhood for baby pink roses, one of Phyllis's favorite flowers, and brought them. They asked if they could put them near her. Grandma Phyllis had beautiful hands and always had her nails done. In death this was no different. Linda, her daughter-in-law had done her nails just a few days earlier and they looked lovely. Upon death, grandma was gently lowered to a flat position (her head had been slightly raised before death) and her hands gracefully lay upon her tummy. The pink roses were placed in her hands. While waiting for the transportation company to arrive anyone who wanted private time with Phyllis had time.

10.1 A Short Checklist

✔ In general, if you are with someone who dies, note the time. If an individual dies in a medical facility this is less important as nursing personnel will note the time. However, loved ones will often want to know and even talk about it, but they would feel uncomfortable talking about it with busy facility personnel. If the death is at home then someone should note the time since that information will be needed for the death certificate. For expected deaths authorities wouldn't question the time, but for unexpected and particularly violent deaths, authorities could question the time of death later.

✔ Not everyone dies a peaceful death like Grandma Phyllis. Unlike the movies, reality is that both the eyes and mouth of the deceased may be open and may not stay closed. Try closing the eyes several times with your finger. If authorized to do so (the deceased is not a stranger or casual acquaintance) the eyes may be taped shut. The mouth may not stay shut because the jaw can become stiff rather fast, depending on the environment. Laying the body flat on the back can help.

✔ If you are responsible for the deceased you will need to produce his or her Social Security number, the name and phone number of the deceased's doctor, and know who to call for the transportation of the body.

Places One May Die

"Played five aces,
Now playing a harp."

— Boot Hill Cemetery tombstone,
Dodge City, Kansas

11.1 Facility

Many people today die in facilities — hospitals, nursing homes, hospices, retirement homes. Mortuaries and hospitals are the only places that will have refrigeration (a morgue) and may allow the body to stay a little longer than the other facilities. Most places only allow four hours. and all of them have some basic "after-death" procedures:

1. **The length of time the body may remain in the facility.**

2. **Disposition of the body.** If there is no family or authorized agent, and no arrangements provided, the body will automatically go to the local county system.

3. **Deceased's possessions.** The family or authorized agent may take the possessions at the time of death or pick them up at a later time as allowed by the facility. If there is a chance of robbery, particularly if the possession is perceived as valuable, the family or authorized agent may want to take possession of anything of value on the deceased's body.

4. **Shroud Pack.** If the body is going to the county or is to be picked up by a transportation company the facility will place the deceased in a "shroud pack" which is a plastic sheet for wrapping the body, wrap a chin-tie that fits on the chin to the top of the head to close the mouth, tie the hands and feet together, place a body tag on the toe, and attach an identification tag onto the plastic sheet.

5. **Authorized Agent File.** Except for a possible Emergency Room situation all facilities will have a file on the deceased that includes who the authorized agent is and how to contact that person.

11.1.1 Hospital

If the death is expected and the deceased's doctor is available to fill out the death certificate, the authorized agent (if not on the site) will be contacted and allowed to proceed. If an unexpected death occurs the body will most likely be sent to the coroner for autopsy. The coroner will sign the death certificate and release the body. This may take several days.

11.1.2 Nursing Home

Unlike a full service hospital there are no surgeries or emergency rooms. Patients enter from referrals such as a hospital, physician's office or retirement home. Unless death is unexpected, the patient's attending physician will fill out the death certificate as provided by either the doctor or mortuary. How the doctor and authorized agent (if not on the site at the time of death) are to be contacted is part of the facility's' procedure.

11.1.3 Hospice

The word "hospice" describes more a process than a place. Hospice is for someone who is going to die, usually within six months. The modern hospice idea originated in England. People who were going to die could go to a place that would provide caring, understanding and professional help the last few months of their lives. Relief of pain and discomfort became the priority rather than trying to "get well" as practiced in hospitals. This idea came to the U.S. after World War II, but didn't catch on until the 1970s.

Hospice care may be within a hospital in a section or wing devoted to hospice. However, as hospital care is becoming a more expensive issue other options are becoming available, such as moving hospice care out of the hospital and into another building just for hospice care. This could be in a house-sized building. Many hospices are donated homes renovated for hospice needs but keeping the warmth of a home. Hospice care also may be provided at a patient's home. Caregivers such as nurses, a doctor, volunteers, social workers and clergy attend to the patient with goods and services arranged as needed.

Because death is expected, the procedure for a doctor (attending physician) filling out the death certificate is usually uncomplicated. The hospice or mortuary will have the forms and the patient's doctor will fill it out.

11.1.4 Retirement Home

Usually these facilities have an age limit and a limit on caring for someone with medical problems. Some have restrictions on old-age dementia. The retiree must be competent mentally and physically. Quite often the retiree lives quite a distance from family and/or an authorized agent. If the retiree dies the facility will contact the authorized agent.

If there is no attending physician to fill out the death certificate or the death is unexpected, the deceased may be sent to the local coroner's office. If not, the facility will expect the authorized agent to arrange disposition. These facilities usually have references for transportation providers and mortuaries if needed. Planning ahead in this situation is an excellent idea.

11.2 Decedent's Home

If the death is unexpected, 911 will need to be called. Paramedics will attempt resuscitation unless there is a "Do Not Resuscitate" form available. Unless there is a doctor to fill out the death certificate the body will be taken to the county coroner. If death is due to homicide or suicide the police will respond.

If the death is expected, the attending physician fills out the death certificate. The physician may not actually be at the home or it might be hard to even contact the physician immediately. A funeral home may be called and they will arrange to pick up the body. The name of the deceased's physician and their Social Security number will be needed. The transportation company contracted by the funeral home will take the information. The funeral home, for a fee, will arrange for a death certificate to be signed. If they are unable to contact the deceased's physician or there is no physician, the funeral home will contact the local coroner's office that will arrange for a physician to sign the death certificate.

The length of time the body may stay in the home depends on the temperature indoors and state laws. Temperature affects the post-death process. The cooler the temperature, the slower the process.

11.3 Outside the Decedent's Home

If a person dies unexpectedly, the body will go to the coroner for an autopsy. When the autopsy is completed and the coroner's office releases the body, it will need to be picked up. Some county coroners' offices may charge a fee for this.

11.3.1 Another Person's Home

If the death is expected or unexpected 911 will be called unless the homeowner is also the authorized agent for the deceased, knows they have on their person a "Do Not Resuscitate" form, and are comfortable with not calling 911. Otherwise the homeowner will definitely want to call 911. If the authorized agent is known (or a family member) to the homeowner, call the agent (or family member) and let them know what has happened. If this information isn't known to the homeowner calling 911 will suffice.

11.3.2 A Public Place

If the person dies alone, hopefully someone will call 911. The body will be sent to the coroner. If you are with a dying person, whether a stranger or someone you know, and if the situation is safe and you feel comfortable, feel free to stay with the dying person. Hold their hand, get your body close to them, look at their face as you talk or let them talk, even when you or another administer first aid. The dying person, particularly if death is unexpected and in a public place, may be afraid, angry or embarrassed. Stranger or not, the dying person may need someone with them.

If you have called 911 or know someone else has, wait with the body since you will be considered a witness. If you are in a desolate place, have no cell phone, and there is little hope of someone else appearing, note the location of the body, lightly cover the face if you wish, but don't use something valuable of your own because you may not get it back from the authorities as it could be labeled "evidence." Find the nearest phone, call 911 and ask if you should wait by the phone. If it is not a safe location explain that to the 911 operator, or go to a safe location first, then call.

Know you did the best you could giving the dying person comfort and respect for the body. The experience may give you sadness, even bad dreams for a time, but eventually you will realize you gave a fellow human being a great gift.

Upon death it is possible there will be urine and bowel debris under the body. If someone dies on your property unexpectedly, when calling 911, ask if you may start to clean up the area, if needed. You may be required to leave it for the authorities. If death is due to a homicide, in addition to the urine and bowel debris there can be blood and body tissue. The authorities will definitely want everything left alone. After the body is removed and the police give the release only then may cleaning commence.

11.4 Outside the Decedent's City, County, State or Country
Here is basic transportation information:

11.4.1 City or County

For body disposition it is still relatively easy to transport the body, either with professional help or on your own, if that state allows non-professional removal assistance. However, a Death Certificate and Transit Permit will be needed in most circumstances (see Part III, "Final Arrangements" for more information),

11.4.2 State

There are two options. The disposition of the remains may take place where the person died, or the remains may be transported to another site. If the deceased was with someone at the time of death, that person, if not the authorized agent or immediate family member, will need to notify someone who can make decisions about the disposition of the remains. If the body is to be moved it is recommended that a professional funeral provider be contacted as embalming may be required as well as knowledge of interstate/intrastate shipping regulations. "Interstate" refers to two or more states and "intrastate" is within the boundaries of one state.

11.4.3 Country

This is called "International Repatriation" and is covered in depth in the chapter called "International Repatriation".

There was a young man at Nunhead
Who awoke in his coffin of lead,
"It is cozy enough,"
He remarked in a huff,
"But I wasn't aware I was dead."

— Early 20th Century limerick
of unknown origin

Airplanes, Ships And Trains

"If you have the need to make a final comment to a departed loved one, you're in luck. The York Group of Houston, Texas has introduced the York Expressions casket that features a special coating on which you can write a final farewell."

— Solitude in Stone newsletter

12.1 Airplanes

If someone dies alone on an airplane, the airline may put down at the nearest airport that can handle the type of plane. It is not unusual, however, for the plane to complete its flight. Airline personnel will go through pockets and carry-on luggage to find pertinent information. Personnel in the cockpit will call ahead to inform the airport of the death. The airline will endeavor to contact someone using the contact phone number used in ticketing and any other information found by airline personnel.

The deceased will be off-loaded from the plane and taken to the local coroner for autopsy. Whoever has been contacted will need to arrange for the transportation of the body once the autopsy is completed. If the deceased has a pre-arrangement with a funeral/ cremation professional that professional may be contacted. Due to the circumstances of the death there will probably be extra charges for the paperwork and transportation not covered in the original contract.

It is not unheard of for the deceased to be either buried or cremated in the local area after the autopsy. This needs to be arranged and the person responsible for the deceased may call their local professional, or one in the area of the burial or cremation, if no pre-arrangement has been done.

12.1.1 Shipment of Human Remains

Most domestic and international airlines ship human remains. Burial of remains is still the choice for many people. There are two circumstances where the shipment of remains on an airplane is a viable option. If the death occurs outside of one's local area the body may be shipped by air back to the home area. The other situation is a funeral/ memorial service to be held in one place with burial in another town, state or country. Proper documentation and shipping container rules and regulations depend on the airline and country. Escorts may accompany the deceased on the same flight. Shipping to another country or shipment of remains into the United States involves additional paperwork and shipping regulations. The cost fluctuates, depending on the airline and country.

12.1.2 Bereavement Fares

Many airlines offer what is called a "bereavement fare," a discounted fare for the person who is escorting the deceased. The discount can be from 15% to 50% off full fare prices. The bereavement fare is only for the escort of the body. Bereavement fares also may be offered for passengers with a death in the family. Some airlines also offer discounts in cases of critical illness in the family. These are viewed as "emergency" flights as the individual has to travel unexpectedly and in a hurry, and are for immediate family only. Each airline has its own pricing and rules. In the case of "emergency" flights the airline may require proof. However, the airlines also feel that it is "good public relations" to put the passenger on the plane. The airlines say that this is not something that is abused by the flying public.

12.2 Ships

There are two parts to most cruises: the sailing itself, (the time one is aboard the ship) and the shore excursions (the time one is on land). If a death occurs onboard a ship the ship's personnel will help arrange for the transfer of the body. Cruise lines may be more comfortable in certain ports because of such factors as having a better working relationship with the port, better facilities and the area's general stability.

12.2.1 On Board

Cruise ships often have the facilities to keep a body for a short period of time and therefore can accommodate the family's wishes. It is not unheard of for the survivor on board to request the body be transported to the final destination, particularly if it is a round-trip cruise. There are no standard rules on this; each situation is dealt with on an individual basis. This situation depends on whether the ship returns to the port of embarkation or company rules, and the wishes of the travel companion or family members. The cruise line is not responsible for the cost incurred in the transportation of the body or accompanying survivors. This can cost thousands of dollars. Trip cancellation insurance that includes evacuation expenses can be bought before the cruise.

Every ship has a large refrigerator that is called the "morgue" and is big enough for two bodies. Usually when a death at sea occurs, the ship contacts its ship's agent (also called the "port" agent) who makes all the legal arrangements. This can include contacting the next-of-kin and preparations for evacuation of the ship at the next port. If no information on the deceased is available the agent will call the travel agency that booked the deceased on the cruise. Cruise consultants suggest travelers give the cruise ship an emergency contact phone number.

12.2.2 On Shore

If a death should occur while one is on shore the survivor(s) will want to contact the port agent. The port agent can be a single person with a phone or a mega-maritime agency, and every port has one. A port agent handles pretty much everything that happens in a harbor/port. A good piece of advice is to always take the name, phone number and address of the port agent any time you get off the ship to go ashore. This information can be found in the material that comes with your ticket and is also usually printed on one of the pages of the daily activities newsletter that is slipped under the door of your cabin each morning.

Not having this bit of information can create a nightmare. Yoko and Fred, a retired married Japanese-American couple, were on their "when-we-retire" cruise. They went ashore at one of the South American ports with a group but they eventually ended up on their own just meandering. They ended up just outside the port town in a small restaurant. Fred, choking on a piece of food, accidentally threw his head backward and struck the wall. He died instantly.

Yoko and some of the restaurant personnel tried to revive Fred but it became apparent to all he was dead. The patrons in the restaurant slipped away and the restaurant staff became somewhat nervous. Yoko spoke no Spanish and they spoke no English. Yoko spied a telephone and asked them in pantomime to call medical authorities. The staff offered Yoko the phone but they would not call anyone.

Yoko kept saying they were Americans and asking if there was an American Consul in the area. Cruises do not require passports and Fred and Yoko, thinking they were smart in not taking their wallets with them on land in case of pick-pockets, had nothing to show the restaurant any identity.

Yoko attempted to call the ship but without knowing Spanish was not successful. Hearing an argument, Yoko turned to see a couple of the restaurant staff move Fred's body outside the restaurant. Yoko dropped the phone and ran to the men, pleading with them to bring the body inside, but they refused. Yoko, by now close to hysteria, had no idea what to do. The ship had sailed. She was alone with a decision to make. Would she stay with Fred's body or try to find help? By now the staff was very nervous and didn't want her to come inside, much less use the phone.

Yoko, crying, angry and frustrated kept mentioning she was American and couldn't she contact someone? A voice finally spoke to her in accented English in the dark. The English speaker turned out to be a niece of the port agent for the cruise company at that port. She had some understanding of his job duties. She also knew why the restaurant staff had appeared to be rather nervous around Yoko. Drug trafficking was a big industry in the area, Asian looking people were rumored to have appeared as drug traffickers. A bizarre bad luck situation.

Yoko was lucky the niece of the port agent was there. He was contacted and started the arrangements for the transfer of Fred's body and Yoko's transportation needs. Yoko and Fred didn't know about port agents or the fact that each port agent's name, phone and address were printed on the daily activity sheets. Know this and remember to copy the information whenever you leave your cruise ship for a shore excursion.

12.3 Trains

An escort may travel with a deceased person on the same train within the United States. A bereavement fare may be available. The person making the arrangements will have to ask and there is no guarantee there will be such a fare.

If a person dies while on the train, at the next scheduled stop the local authorities will be contacted.

If you are with someone who dies you may contact the conductor immediately and find out where the train will stop. Using either a cell phone or the phone on the train you will be able to call people you need.

The deceased will undoubtedly be taken to the coroner for an autopsy. That will give you time to make arrangements. Cremation can be done locally and the cremains (cremated remains) taken home with you. If burial back home is wished, a funeral professional will be needed to make the travel arrangements.

International Repatriation

"When it's time to go, should we just laugh?"

— Truman Capote,
author and playwright

International repatriation is the transfer of a human body from one country to another. People of all ages traveling on business, vacation or living abroad die away from their country of citizenship. Notification of the death is the beginning of a complex, paper laden process.

If you travel frequently, it is a good idea to let someone know whom to call if a death occurs. Another nugget of knowledge is that if you buy flight insurance on a per-flight basis, tell someone. Insurance companies don't always contact the beneficiaries to tell them they are due settlements. They may wait for somebody to call them.

It is certainly worth the effort to have final arrangements (including what to do if one dies away from home) planned prior to one's death. Carry an authorized agent type of card with that person's name and phone number on it. If you really want to be prepared, have the contact names and phone numbers in the language of the country you are in.

13.1 Questions to be Asked and Answered:

13.1.1 How is the decedent's body returned to the U.S.?

At the time of death local law authorities and the Consul General at the nearest United States Embassy or Consulate need to be informed. A family member or survivor will be notified. Whoever has the authority to make the arrangements (the next-of-kin or authorized agent) will need to call a funeral provider in the United States, who is called the "consignee" or "receiver of human remains." The consignee will call the nearest Consul General in the United States for repatriation instructions (return of the body). The consignee must arrange for the necessary preparations and documentation, usually working with professionals in the country where the deceased died, as well as the United State Embassy.

International repatriation can be a rather costly and complex transaction. An example is the price of transferring the body. If a common carrier (such as an airplane) is used the fee is based and calculated on freight weight pounds, not the price per ticket. If there has been no pre-planning of this situation and the survivor (person responsible for the remains) is not with the deceased, it could take as long as two weeks for the remains to leave a foreign country. In a third world country the process could take as long as three weeks to release the remains.

An interesting note — A few U.S. Army bases outside the United States have their own embalmers who are part of the U.S. Army Graves & Registration Department. They generally embalm (1) war casualties (2) where available, family members of U.S. service people on active duty (3) residing diplomats (4) special circumstance cases. G&R is not intended for general public use although if you die abroad in an Army hospital you will, in all likelihood, be embalmed on the premises by U.S. embalmers.

13.1.2 How is international repatriation paid?
- The survivor pays the consignee for the transfer with cash, check or credit card.
- The survivor establishes credit with the United States Embassy in the foreign country where death occurred.

- The survivor arranges for credit with a bank, which will then contact the consignee or the United States Embassy in the country where the death occurred.
- The survivor orders U.S. funds to be wired to the consignee.
- The survivor, if short of funds or credit, considers a less expensive alternative type of disposition such as:
  1. Cremation with no memorial or funeral service.
  2. Burial at sea. Many times, this is a government-provided service. However, arranging it may be very time consuming.
  3. Immediate burial where the death occurred.
  4. Body donation for scientific research (including organ donation if one wishes).

13.1.3 What if the deceased is cremated?

If the survivor is with the deceased at the time of death, he or she needs to notify the closest U.S. Embassy or Consulate and then make arrangements with a local funeral provider for the disposition. The United States Embassy or Consulate should be available to assist and guide United States citizens traveling abroad. Additionally, the survivor can expect to personally take the cremains (cremated remains) with them if they so choose. Otherwise, a registered courier is a viable option to transfer cremains.

If the survivor is not with the deceased, the survivor will contact and pay a reputable consignee who will transfer funds to the United States Embassy or Consulate and/or funeral provider in the country where the death occurred. It is legal to mail cremains, although not all funeral providers will do so because of possible litigation problems. On occasion, a funeral provider will mail the cremains and the package not arrive. Thus the sender is liable for the loss. Advice for anyone mailing cremains: obtain written permission from the person who will be receiving the cremains and document the mail transaction.

13.1.4 How does one find a good international repatriation consignee?

- The firm should have a history of superior service and reputation.
- The firm should have expertise in international repatriation. Ask how many foreign transfers they have arranged, both body return and cremation.
- Is the firm capable of handling the requested arrangements?
- Suggestion: many funeral providers have a referral system in other countries. The firms network with firms in other countries.

13.1.5 How does a person pre-plan this kind of situation?

Find a reputable funeral provider and discuss your situation. Ask questions and get all the facts and possible prices. Because airline freight charges change almost daily and one doesn't know what country one might die in, it is not possible to pre-finance, to-the-penny, an international repatriation before it happens. However, by talking to a professional provider you can receive an idea of the cost, what the situation entails and what documents are needed. Take your survivor, the person who will be the one to contact the consignee, with you. If that person doesn't live in the area make sure the situation and your wishes are fully discussed, agreed upon, and written down. Now is the time to discuss if repatriation is affordable or if burial or cremation should be in the country where the death occurred, and how the service charges will be afforded and billed.

If you do not have a relative or authorized agent and you care what happens to your remains, then you need to work out an arrangement including financing with a consignee and sign the needed documents allowing the consignee to also become the authorized agent. The consignee's name and phone number should be on your person at all times. You would also be doing the U.S. Embassy a big favor in time and energy spent trying to find a survivor. Your government would be grateful!

13.1.6 What happens if a person dies alone in a foreign country?

Once the body is found, it will be reported to the local law enforcement agency that will contact the local U.S. Embassy. A local funeral provider in that country may be contacted. The Embassy and/or funeral provider will try to reach a survivor.

13.1.7 What if you are with someone who dies in a foreign country?

- Stranger: if you happen to come upon a dead person in a foreign country it is your decision whether or not to inform local law enforcement. Not knowing the local language and customs could be a hindrance when trying to report a death. If you know that the dead person is American, the local U.S. Embassy or Consulate should be contacted.

- Friend: if you are traveling with someone you know call the local law enforcement and the Consul General at the nearest U.S. Embassy. If you know the person's family you may want to call the survivor(s) and personally let them know what has happened. If you are not the person authorized to make arrangements it will be up to you to decide if you stay on to ensure that arrangements are processed as soon as possible. You are not legally responsible for anything, so this is a personal decision you will be making.

- Spouse/Mate/Offspring: as with a friend, one needs to call local law authorities and the Consul General at the nearest U.S. Embassy. If you are a spouse you have the legal right to make arrangements for a body transfer, burial or cremation. If you are not married you need an authorized agent document and even that may not prevent some problems. Not all countries recognize an unmarried partner even with the proper documentation. If your minor child dies in a foreign country without you present, you will need to talk to the Embassy or Consulate. If you are with your child and want the body brought back to your home you will need a U.S. consignee.

13.2 Three Tips

- People traveling alone should always carry phone numbers of the next of kin.

- Solo travelers let your tour company escorts know where pertinent documents are packed.

- Trip cancellation insurance is highly recommended. Read the policy carefully!

An interesting side note — some countries engage in what Americans would call "bribery" and although not officially part of international repatriation it can occasionally pop up in repatriation negotiations. The U.S. Embassy that is handling the repatriation would be aware if any form of bribery is used in that particular country.

PART III
FINAL ARRANGEMENTS

Lester suffered a heart attack and died during the top of the ninth inning of the first game of a double-header with the St. Louis Cardinals. He was sitting in the front row of the right-field bleachers. He had sat there during virtually every weekend home game for the last 45 years or so.

Lester and his lifelong friend Marvin were legends within the legend of the Wrigley Field bleachers. The two men had been attending ballgames together for nearly five decades.

Losing season after season Marv would sit bare chested, mouthing a cigar that he never lit before the 7th inning, next to Les. He called Les, who was two years younger, "Junior."

Marv was gruff; Les was quiet. The most emotion they showed was to curse under their breaths at a bad play. Marv muttered more than Les, and kept score. If the Cubs lost, he threw away the scorecard. Les bit his nails and, under extreme baseball duress, could be seen to throw his hands up in the air.

Marv, a messenger, died a couple of years before Lester, of pneumonia at the age of 59. Lester, also at the age of 59, a mailroom supervisor, has joined him. The bleacher regulars joined his family to bid him farewell at his wake and funeral.

— American Funeral Director Magazine

What A Way To Go!

"I don't care what my obituary says, because I'll be dead. If I'm not dead, that would be a great column."

— Dave Barry, columnist

14.1 A Short History of Death Customs in the United States

Prior to the 17th century, various tribes of people, later to become known as American Indians, populated the area which became The United States of America. Death customs included both burial and cremation, and the rituals and practices attending to death were as varied as the tribes. Today many of the tribes still practice death rituals as well as combine their tribe's rituals with non-tribal religious practices.

In America during the 1600s both the Puritans of the north, New England, and the Anglicans of the south, buried their dead primarily in cemeteries. This was an English custom brought to America by the two English religions. There was a difference in monuments with the Puritans favoring simple tombstones (also called "headstones") with a winged death head or skull, and the Anglican favoring cherubs (baby angels) and angels.

European public cemeteries were considered humble places and used by the poor and unknown. The wealthier classes buried their dead in private cemeteries, usually on family grounds. Royalty and the well connected were buried in the church. Large elaborate tombstones of Europe gave way in eastern America to smaller but elegant monuments. To be buried outdoors, instead of in the church, was preferred. Other religions arrived in America as well, bringing their traditions.

Africans arrived in America in chains as slaves for the South. Indentured or free Blacks in the north were not usually from Africa.

The African cultures, in general, did not have a history of an elaborate tombstone but both burial and cremation were used in Africa. Wealthy southern plantation owners and their slaves were buried on plantation grounds, family and slave each having their own plantation cemetery. The plantation owner often would have elaborate tombstones; the slave was not allowed such memorial tribute. Efforts to convert the slaves to Christianity were partially successful; however, African slaves often did maintain their African religious practices hidden from their white owners.

The black slave, caught between two cultures, their own and their master's, turned their energy towards the burial itself. The black slaves did not have the right to organize their own rituals for death. However, as time passed, distinctive rituals and practices did appear and evolve. The African slaves were originally of different tribes in Africa with different death traditions, but generally speaking, in the new world both the "slave state" slaves and the free black people of the north followed the predominant religions' death practices to a point. In 1796 the First African Methodist Episcopal Zion Church was founded and continues today.

Denied so much in life the slaves were able to mourn their dead quite openly as opposed to the "discreet mourning" often practiced by the white population. A wonderful example today is the New Orleans funeral march complete with New Orleans jazz.

Prior to the rush West by immigrants and American-born pioneers, southwestern America was under the influence of the Hispanic Catholic church. Burial and elaborate tombstones proliferated. Indian tribes were introduced to elaborate tombstones along with a new religion. Upheaval in their culture and lives ensued with death rituals becoming hidden from outsiders.

The 1800s saw tremendous human mobility, and private burial was eventually abandoned late in the century, both in the cities and the countryside. Ideas of sanitation and public health were under discussion. The words "churchyard" and "graveyard" were replaced with the non-sectarian "cemetery" as burial became non-secular and under government control. Today, some states will allow a "home" burial, but due to rigid environmental laws, most homes do not have enough land requirements, nor do people have the money for the private burial accouterments as regulated by the government. Franklin D. Roosevelt, U.S. President, was buried in such a manner at his family estate in upstate New York, as was the murdered son of entertainer Bill Cosby.

Up until the 20th century, when a person died the family laid the deceased out on a board between two chairs draped with a cloth. The family washed the body and the mouth was wedged shut. Coins were often used to keep the eyes shut. Thus the body was laid out for mourners to visit during the wake. During warm summer months it was not unusual to find tubs of ice placed beneath the boards and body. The local cabinetmaker was pressed into service to make a coffin that was smaller than the current large rectangular shape. The coffined body was taken to the graveyard where a sexton (minor church official) or friends dug the grave. The mourners would fill the grave and the service would be over.

Cremation, thousands of years old, was practiced in Europe and Asia. American Indians and Catholics did not believe in cremation. As Christianity, became more popular, burial became the norm and cremation was considered "pagan". Ancient cremation had been done outside with no enclosed chamber and that tradition disappeared in Europe during 1873, when Professor Brunetti of Italy produced a dependable burning chamber. Three years later the first American crematorium was built in Pennsylvania. Early crematoriums were owned and operated by a cremation society. The impetus for cremation came from Protestant clergy, who desired to reform burial practices, and the medical profession, concerned with health conditions around early cemeteries. By the early 20th century there were over 50 crematories in the nation.

The 20th century saw the emergence of for-profit and non-profit memorial organizations, which allow mourners to mourn the death even if the body itself is not present. Today the word "memorial" is used, often interchangeably, with the word "funeral" as the body may or may not be present.

Well into the 20th century people were dying primarily at home. It was the family's responsibility to prepare the body for burial, and often times the responsibility also included the burial. Post World War I saw the change with people dying outside the home, mostly in hospitals. The modern funeral business evolved with the body under the care of the funeral practitioner. Today the re-emergence of the "family style" funeral makes it possible, under certain conditions and in certain states, to consider non-professionals such as family and friends to be responsible for transportation, preparation, and in some cases, burial of the body.

A very ancient practice, mummification, is making a comeback of sorts, while a very new high tech procedure of cryonics or freezing has caught the attention of the rich, famous and just plain curious. Cremated remains may be sent to outer space, sent deep into the sea or worn as jewelry.

It is often said funerals are for the living, not for the dead. The survivors are the ones to grieve, to want some kind of closure. Often some kind of ceremony is wanted or needed. The tending of and grieving over a loved one's remains is an intimate experience. Paying homage to the famous is often expected. People in all walks of life have different ideas on how these things should be done.

There are a lot of choices out there. Let's take a look...

14.2 Components of a Funeral

In the United States there are choices as to what kind of, if any, gatherings and rituals are to be done at the time of death. Funerals are like weddings. They can be complicated and expensive. Will a lot of people be attending or is it a simple affair with just a few people? Both involve people at an emotional time in their lives.

Funerals can be religious or secular. They are held in places of worship, outdoors, in homes, at businesses — the list goes on. Humans are just as creative with their funerals as they are with their weddings. Religion can dictate when, where and how a funeral service will proceed. Some funerals are seen as an extension of a business's public relations such as when a business president or CEO dies. Embedded within funerals are several components. Not all funerals use all the components.

14.2.1 Visitation/Viewing is a ritual wherein the body of the deceased is arranged in a coffin so that the living may visit the deceased. These visitations range from formal State affairs where thousands of people will simply file past the deceased to small informal visitations where the living may stop, look, talk to, even touch the departed. Visitations/Viewings are held in mortuaries, houses of worship, public buildings or at cemeteries that have visitation accommodations. Visitation/Viewings may run several days or be relegated to a certain time, often just before the funeral service itself

14.2.2 The funeral service is the actual gathering of people in honor of the deceased with the body present. Depending on religion, local custom, condition of the body, and wishes of the deceased and survivors, the coffin may be open or closed. The service may or may not include a formal line of attendees walking up to the coffin for a final viewing. It may be quite simple, at the site of the grave, called a "grave-side service."

14.2.3 A memorial service is an alternative funeral service, with the body not present. It can be as formal as a grand funeral or a small gathering of people in a home or on a hill just for people to cry and remember together for a bit.

14.2.4 Body disposition services can be on land, air or at sea. There are five different ways for the disposition of the body in the United States: burial (including entombment and burial-at-sea), cremation, mummification, cryonics and body/organ donation.

14.2.5 A Wake is a gathering of people either before a funeral or after, often includes food and drink and can be a way for people to relax a bit during this time of stress, loss and sadness.

WAKE

Tell all my mourners
To mourn in red —
Cause there ain't no sense
In my bein' dead.

— Langston Hughes, writer,
Collected Poems of Langston Hughes

The Business Of Death

"The care of 200 millions of dollars is too great
a load for any brain or back to bear. It is enough
to kill a man. There is no pleasure to be got out of it as
an offset — no good of any kind.
I have no real gratification of enjoyment of any
sort more than my neighbor on the next block
who is worth only half a million."

— William Vanderbilt,
businessman, upon his deathbed

15.1 Professional Providers

There are usually two types of people making funeral arrangements with a professional funeral director: those who are making arrangements for someone who has died, or people making arrangements for themselves for the future. More people are making arrangements for others than themselves at present, but the number of personal pre-planners is growing.

Historically this wasn't always the case. Before the 21st century many societies thought it quite proper, indeed it was almost mandatory, for an individual to let others know what was to be done upon their death. It was not unusual for people to actually compose their own death words: tombstone inscription, what was to be included during the funeral, and any literature for posterity. The last was usually reserved for the wealthy, the well-known, and church officials. This was also true for Native American tribal chiefs.

In modern times this custom has become much less so, although there are individuals and groups who will inform one another what to write or say. Today, as stated, there are a lot of options available, and people are breaking with past traditions and starting new ones. In order to know what is available one needs to spend time and effort to find all the options.

The use of a professional funeral provider is rather recent. Up until well into the 20th century it was the responsibility of the family and friends to ready the body for burial since the deceased usually died at home. The local cabinetmaker could make a coffin if the family wished, and the family could hire a horse and buggy to transport the body if needed. The wealthy could afford to have whatever they wished and the poor often had to depend on the church. It was with the rise of the middle class after World War II that the professional funeral business emerged. Death and burial responsibilities were removed from the home.

Today funeral providers can provide all goods and services. If it is a smaller business the professional will have a network of service/goods providers. When individuals are planning for their own funerals, they have more time, can choose exactly what they wish, and usually are not affected by grief.

However, the majority of people seeking the services of a funeral provider are there on behalf of another who has died. Stress, grief and unethical practices can make a hard situation even worse. However, like much of life, it certainly is better to have some knowledge and some preparation for life's situations, including death.

In France there are funeral supermarkets. They are large stores where one can go in and purchase that which is needed or wanted—flowers, casket, music—it's all there. In the U.S. there are no funeral supermarkets, although there are discount casket warehouses and Internet sites for those who wish to buy the casket direct. So how does one find out what is available and then make an informed choice? Presented here is generic funeral information that can be used by either those planning their own last rites or for others who are making the arrangements for someone who has died.

15.1.1 How to Find a Good Funeral Home/Mortuary

Obviously if you have had prior experience with a professional funeral service and were pleased you will probably discuss your own wishes and needs with the same business. If you do not have any experience here is a list of suggestions:

If you know someone you can call who has had experience, call him or her for advice. If it is in the middle of the night in a medical facility you may or may not be able to get a referral from the staff. The non-medical staff of a facility is usually off the premises at night. If you don't already know the policy of the facility on how long a body may remain on the premises, you will need to ask.

If there is nobody to ask, or the death occurs at home, you will need to use the Yellow Pages in the telephone directory. Look under "Funeral," "Mortuary," "Cremation" or "Crematory." Pick one and call. Someone should be on duty. If no answer try another. Further arrangements can wait until the next day, although you should ask the cost of the transportation and storage until you do meet with the provider. If you change providers there will be a charge by the first provider.

Visit those funeral providers recommended to you or selected from the telephone book. Also pay close attention to the following:

1. **Ask questions.** Are the staff members with which you speak accommodating, informative, well groomed, caring?

2. **Is the place neat and clean?** Are there old flowers lying about? Is the place sloppy and cluttered? Check their licensure, community involvement, and attitude. This is a professional business; therefore, does the staff act professional and businesslike?

3. **Discuss all options.** If you have particular wishes see if they are willing and able to accommodate them.

4. **Discuss cost.** Get the general price list, which is legally mandated. Every item of service and merchandise must be listed. Make sure you and the funeral director have a clear understanding of when and how your funeral is to be paid.

15.1.2 What It Will Cost

The economy of the area, religious and ethnic customs, family preferences, community practices, and traditions have an effect on cost. Four separate and distinct categories of charges make up the cost of a funeral:

1. Those which specifically involve the funeral director, including professional services and those of the staff; the use of the facility and equipment; the casket/interment receptacle and other items of merchandise.

2. Those dealing with the disposition of the body. If earth-interred, there is the cost of the grave space (cemetery plot) and charges for opening and closing the grave. If cremated, there is a charge for the actual cremation. Urns are an extra cost. For above ground disposition, there is the cost of the mausoleum crypt.

3. Those for memorialization or remembrance such as a monument or marker for the grave or a niche for the urn of cremated remains.

4. Those miscellaneous expenses, also known as "cash advances," paid by the family directly or through the funeral director. This includes such things as clergy honorarium and other religious-related costs, flowers, music, newspaper death notices, limousines (if not included in the price of the funeral) and transportation of the body, if needed. The mortuary can also provide certified copies of the death certificate, which is needed for a number of different legal and financial issues following a death.

Today federal law requires all mortuaries to provide a general price list that itemizes all services and merchandise. This way one can sit down with a professional and not only learn the cost of goods and services but also what the various goods and services actually mean and what legal documents, forms and personal information are needed.

15.1.3 How To Pay For A Funeral

Final arrangements, whether they are simple and locally done or the much more complex international repatriation will cost something. Even when making the final arrangements yourself, there are things to pay for as noted in these chapters. Even if the deceased has left some kind of insurance to help pay for the final arrangements, quite often those funds will not be released in time for payment before the disposition of the dead person's remains. That means someone is going to have to pay out of pocket, at least until the insurance has been processed and paid out to the beneficiary or estate. If you sign the insurance policy over to the funeral provider check to see if you have money coming back to you.

CASH

Cash can be used in the U.S. but make sure you get receipts, on the spot. Don't wait for them to be mailed. Depending on what you are buying it could mean lots of cash, up to thousands of dollars. In general, it is not advisable or practical to engage in such large cash transactions. ATMs only allow $500 withdrawals per 24-hour period.

Purchasing goods and services in a foreign country is more complicated. If you are on the site you may be able to use U.S. dollars, although, in many countries it would be necessary to convert to local currency. Because international repatriation usually involves a professional you could pay that part directly (in the United States).

PERSONAL CHECK

Personal checks are not always accepted. Naturally if the final arrangements were local, you, as the survivor, would have no problem with a check, as it would be local. But if you are paying out-of-state there might be a "hold" put on the check of 3-5 working days while it is being ascertained it is good for the payment. You could call your bank and they could speak to the provider. Expect to pay for that long distance call.

Using personal checks for payment outside the U.S. is highly unlikely. If one has a problem cashing a check out-of-state, you can imagine how difficult it would be out of the country. Again, because international repatriation requires a professional provider, you would be dealing with the provider here in the U.S. However, if you are in the country where the death occurred and are planning cremation, you probably will still have a problem writing a U.S. check.

TRAVELER'S CHECKS

Traveler's checks can be used inside and outside the U.S. One problem is if the traveler's checks are in the deceased's name and not yours. You won't be able to use them if your name is not on them. However, if you plan to travel to the site of the death, traveler's checks might be useful for you to purchase in your own name.

If you are traveling with someone who dies it is beneficial to have the type of traveler's checks that allow either you or the other person to use them. Before setting off on a trip ask your bank.

BANK DRAFT/TRANSFER

This is more complicated and not useful for all situations. When final arrangements involve anything that needs to be paid outside the local area, money can be transferred to the person or place where needed. Professional providers in your local area would be most familiar with these arrangements and the paying of bills. Often the person responsible will work out a contract where the professional provider will be paid all funds by the person responsible and the provider will distribute the funds as needed. In international repatriation the professional, (the "consignee") is responsible for all arrangements and a good professional will know how to do this.

If you are planning to go to the site you may want to have your bank transfer funds for you to a bank at the death site. That is something you and your bank will need to discuss, preferably prior to any expensive family travels abroad.

CREDIT CARD
The plus side for credit cards is that they can be used pretty much all over the world and they are "instant cash" when needed. The down side is not all funeral/body disposition providers take credit cards or your credit limit on the card is not high enough to meet all the expenses.

15.1.4 Questions and Answers
Do I have to buy everything from the funeral provider?
No. Many people buy their own cemetery plot, crypt or niche, even multiples for a mate or whole family. Buying your own or someone else's resting place means you have to be sure that it is where you want it to be, and if for yourself, there will be someone to carry out your wishes. Discount casket businesses are popping up in the U.S. now that funeral providers can no longer charge handling fees for caskets purchased outside the funeral home. Make sure you know what you want: quality and look-a-likes are issues to keep in mind. Miscellaneous expenses such as clergy, flowers, music and newspaper death notices (obituary) are not required to be arranged and paid through the funeral provider.

Why can there be such a difference in price among providers?
There are several reasons. Excluding the church-related providers, funeral providers are primarily a for-profit business. The cost of their overhead will have an impact on their prices. The bigger the physical plant and the more in-house services offered the bigger the price. Due to extensive marketing, some providers have become quite well known. Demand for

their services is high, therefore their prices may be higher. Another factor is the socio-economic status of the clients. Providers in lower income neighborhoods tend to have lower prices. Any ethical funeral provider is glad to answer questions and provide a price list upon request.

How to pay for it?

Realize that "goods and services" starts with picking up the body and ends when anything connected to the execution of the funeral are completed, including post funeral goods and services such as placement of the grave marker. As already noted, payment may be requested in cash, credit card, check or money order. Some providers want payment up front. This is particularly true of crematoriums, mortuaries in poor neighborhoods and cemeteries dealing with the public directly.

What about pre-paying for final arrangements?

The industry itself maintains there are several reasons _for_ pre-paying:
- It's ok to pre-pay, just choose carefully.
- If you don't pre-pay, the price may keep going up. If you do pre-pay, you can get the price frozen with "guaranteed" plan.
- Advance planning gives you an opportunity to let your family know what kind of funeral you want.
- Pre-paying avoids having to make decisions at a time of grief.
- If you are about to enter a nursing home, the nursing home will expect you to have funds set aside for your death arrangements.

Anti-industry organizations provide reasons _not_ to pre-pay:
- While it always pays to plan ahead, it rarely pays to pay ahead.
- The mortuary could go out of business before you die.
- If the mortuary is sold, the new owner may not honor the prices or quality of goods shown by a prior owner.

- If you were to move, perhaps to be with an adult child in another area, you might not be able to transfer your funds without a penalty.

What about Social Security and Veterans' benefits?

Social Security will reimburse the surviving spouse of eligible decedents in the amount of $255.00. There is an allowance from the Veterans Administration for eligible decedents. You will need to call both the Social Security Administration and Veterans Affairs office for information. When interviewing possible funeral providers ask about these benefits.

Does a body have to be embalmed for a funeral?

No. There are exceptions, which are listed below. Otherwise, if the viewing/funeral is held within a week of death, there should be no problem.

The embalming process was brought to the United States from Europe and became common during the Civil War in the 1860s. Soldiers far away from home were dying and doctors were getting many requests from soldiers' families to have their war dead transported home. This could take many days during the summer, which would render the bodies unsightly and foul smelling. The doctors' dilemma was how to preserve the body long enough for the trip home.

Embalming is the process of preparing the body so that it can be held for the service and so that survivors can have an opportunity to take their leave of the person who died. It primarily involves hygiene: bathing, shaving, shampooing, etc., then preservatives and disinfecting chemicals are injected into the vascular system to replace the blood.

There are times when embalming is mandatory, such as when transporting the body from one state or one country to another. Loved ones often request embalming and cosmetology (hair and make up) services when the deceased has died from disease or trauma and visitation/viewing is desired.

Is an autopsy always performed after death?

No. An autopsy, the examination of a dead body by the coroner's office, is not done when the cause of death is known and a doctor is able to sign the death certificate. When a person dies unexpectedly or the death becomes a police matter an autopsy is mandated. There is no way one can plan their final arrangements and know for certain if an autopsy will be needed.

Can there be a viewing after an autopsy?

Yes. Mortuary personnel are fully familiar with practices to prepare bodies after autopsy.

15.2 Independent / Non-professional Arrangements

This does not mean a do-it-yourself cremation or burial. Professionals are needed always for cremation and for most burials. The essential elements of an independent arrangement are filling out and filing the forms, preparing and transporting the body for burial or cremation and doing tasks such as newspaper obituaries, formal/informal decorations and creating announcements.

15.2.1 Before You Decide

Does your state permit a "Do-it-yourself" funeral?

Some states insist a funeral director sign and file documents. A few states severely restrict or prohibit family-style funerals.

Who is going to be held responsible?

The regulations in most states will probably require that the person who assumes responsibility for the body must carry out the funeral arrangements according to the state health department guidelines. Make sure you have someone to do this if you are planning a family-style funeral.

In states that designate the next-of-kin family as having the responsibility for the funeral, it will take specific written permission (by the deceased prior to death) to have someone outside the family handle the arrangements. The authorized agent can be used here.

What do I need in support?

It takes four to six people to share the emotional and physical burdens when a group takes care of the physical requirements of the body such as washing and dressing, as well as transporting the body.

When should I not consider this option?

- If use of a facility such as a mortuary is desired.
- If the deceased died from a highly contagious disease. Human remains from a contagious disease (and disinterred remains) must be shipped in hermetically (air tight) and permanently sealed caskets and the medical examiner must be notified.
- The deceased or family desires the body to be embalmed.
- Transporting the body interstate or into the U.S. from another country (which may require embalming).

What if I die outside my home?

If it is unexpected and your body ends up at a hospital or coroner's office, the proper documents are produced (in a state that allows this option) your authorized agent or next-of-kin would be able to claim the body. Do be aware that individuals in these facilities may be reluctant to release the body so make sure your agent or family members have the proper documentation.

If the death is expected and at a medical facility, to insure there are no mistakes, make sure your final arrangements are part of the information in the patient's "Plan of Care." Let the facility know, before death, of this arrangement. Have the proper documentation.

What is the proper documentation?

- **Death Certificate** – consists of family history section and a medical section to be filled out by a physician.
- **Disposition-Transit Permit** – (called by different names in

different states) must be filled out and filed with whom-ever the state mandates. It is needed for transport and body disposition.

- **Cremation Permit** – if the body is to be cremated, some states require this. Who needs to sign it depends on the individual's home state.
- **Authorized Agent** – the person responsible. Have picture identification available. This option definitely has to be a "group" decision since more than one person needs to help. The small book, *The Family Funeral* (see "Resources") is a good place to start when researching your options.

15.3 Funeral and Memorial Societies

Funeral and memorial societies are for-profit and non-profit organizations that an individual joins by filling out a form and paying a one-time membership fee. Some societies have annual dues or solicit contributions from time to time. In addition to providing a wide range of funeral planning information, a society often contracts for final arrangements with a funeral provider for certain goods and services at a discount for members. If a contract is not possible, a society will survey the funeral providers in an area and make price information available to members.

Most memorial society members choose an immediate burial, immediate cremation, or body donation to a medical school. By planning a memorial service without the body present, costs should be around $1,000 in most areas if you or the society have done careful price shopping.

The most well known non-profit society in the United States is FAMSA-FCA (Funeral and Memorial Societies of America - Funeral Consumer Alliance), which has a membership of 145 local autonomous memorial societies throughout the U.S. This organization was started in 1963 after the publication of Jessica Mitford's book, *The American Way of Death*, which described the U.S. funeral industry in highly critical terms.

Each affiliate contracts with local mortuaries for the following services at a set price for its members:

Direct Cremation. There is no funeral service; the body goes directly to the mortuary, prepared for cremation and is cremated.

Direct Burial. There is no funeral service; the body goes directly to the mortuary, is prepared for burial, transported to cemetery and buried. The cost of the plot itself is separate and not included in the society contract.

Burial with Service. There is a funeral service and burial. The cost of the plot itself is separate.

The procedure is to pick the provider and plan that you wish, fill out the "pre-arrangement" form (this is information needed for the death certificate), and return the form, with the society's fee. Please note that the prices contracted with the mortuaries are only for each local society. Therefore there can be price differences with different societies.

The society will send you an "Instructions to Mortuary" sheet. Look it over to make sure all is correct. Keep a copy and send the other two copies to the society. They will send the original to the mortuary, which will send a card saying "Yes, received."

This non-profit organization is not to be confused with for-profit businesses that use the word "society" in their advertising. Critics of for-profit societies say their fees tend to be the same or higher than market-driven retail prices found at mortuaries. Usually the for-profits have one arrangement with different payment plans. Additional goods and services may be provided for with additional costs such as a travel option and relocation. "Cremation societies" are becoming more and more prevalent around the country.

If you are responsible for someone's final arrangements, that person would have had to let you know before death of society membership, so documents pertaining to that membership would be readily available to you.

15.3.1 Questions and Answers
What if I change my mind?
The society suggests waiting a week to make sure. Then if you want to change your plans or mortuaries, the paperwork can be done again.

Should I pre-pay for my funeral?
Memorial societies do not provide any direct funeral services. Any advance arrangements must be made with a participating mortuary. The society recommends pre-paying if the consumer is elderly, alone, sick, know they won't be moving and have only a short time to live.

What if I move out of the area?
The membership is transferred to the society in the new area at no charge or for a modest transfer fee.

What if I die outside my society's area?
As a memorial society member, you are entitled to the benefits of membership in the area served by another society. Survivors should contact the nearest society for details and the names of cooperating mortuaries, even if your body is to be returned to a home location for burial. Handling and transportation of the deceased would not be part of the society benefits.

How are the rates determined?
If only one funeral provider in the area is contracted with a society, there is no competition and therefore only one price. In remote areas, cost-of-living often is higher, so cost-of-death is higher. The rates could differ due to the socio-economic level of the community where the provider is located.

There are also for-profit memorial and/or cremation societies that may be regional or national. The non-profit societies say the for-profits often charge as much or more than standard funeral providers. Some for-profit societies, such as a cremation society, state that they can be cheaper since the consumer would not be dealing with a "middle person" such as a funeral director.

For any funeral/cremation/memorial society check to see if Social Security and/or Veterans' death benefits (if applicable to you) may be used and how that reimbursement is handled.

HISTORICAL NOTE:
The word "undertaker" originally applied to
the person who "undertook" the
necessary tasks for burial of the dead.

Cemeteries

"Everyday, in our office, we deal with death.
It's what we do."

— Devin Burgoyne,
cemetery plot salesman

When the United States was created human remains were buried everywhere. There were family plots on family property; property next to churches was reserved for people who qualified by race and religion for burial; Native Americans had sacred areas, and immigrants on the move were buried where they died. Eventually burial regulations surfaced and burial places were defined and regulated by government.

Today cemeteries may be related to a church, if not in the literal sense of physically being next to the church, but are administered by a church or department controlled by a church. There are also secular cemeteries such as Forest Lawn in California, made famous through the novel and film *The Loved One*. It is a top tourist destination.

Because cremation is becoming popular, more cemeteries are able to provide space for the disposition of a body, or have an area reserved for cremated remains. Cemeteries may be nonprofit or for profit.

There are two types of cemeteries: those that are strictly cemeteries and those that have a mortuary on the grounds of the cemetery. While the difference between the two is becoming blurred, the basic difference is that a cemetery is for the final disposition of human remains while a mortuary prepares the body for final disposition.

Unless a person dies at home and a physician signs the death certificate stating that death was of natural causes, the dead body will need to be moved from a hospital, hospice or coroner's office in a relatively short time accompanied by the proper documentation. Unless you are doing a "do-it-yourself" funeral, the body needs to be transported to a mortuary. Medical facilities most likely will have a social worker or patient advocate whom you can ask for suggestions for funeral providers.

Mortuaries that do not have their own cemeteries may go through a burial space broker. If the consumer has a particular cemetery in mind, it is important to make sure the mortuary is willing and able to facilitate final wishes with that cemetery. Please note at some cemeteries the consumer does not purchase the plot as property in fee (own the land itself, in this case the plot) but the consumer owns the right to interment. You will want to ask when researching or making arrangements.

Here are some things to consider when shopping for cemetery products and services.

16.1 How to Determine Which Cemetery To Use

Whether you are choosing for yourself or another person start by seeking general cemetery information and based upon this knowledge you will be able to visit cemeteries as an informed consumer. If you are using the services of a professional funeral provider you still may want to learn about the cemetery he or she recommends. If you are simply learning about cemeteries in general a reputable funeral provider would be able to suggest cemeteries and answer your questions. Ask friends and family of their experiences.

Another way to find cemeteries is to look in the phone book in the yellow pages under "Cemeteries." Another avenue is to call your local memorial society for a recommendation. A person's religion often dictates which cemetery one may wish to use. A Catholic, for example, may find it important to be in a cemetery administered by the Catholic Church.

16.1.1 Being An Informed Consumer

Once you have picked the cemetery (or cemeteries) you are interested in, visit them. Walk around and ask questions. You want to know how long the cemetery has been in business and obtain evidence of having a maintenance trust fund. Cemeteries have to take care of the graves and common areas, and this maintenance costs money. When purchasing a product or service from a cemetery part of that money will go into a maintenance fund. The interest from such funds, which are mandated by the state, is to cover cemeterymaintenance costs. A cemetery should be able to provide records on these funds and a good program for the perpetual upkeep of the cemetery.

There are many cemeteries that are 100 years old or older. Quite often they are rather small and unstaffed. Some are considered historical sites and are there for tourists and/or future generations of the buried ancestors to visit. Some are full and do not permit further burials. It is not uncommon to have an individual or a group voluntarily maintaining the cemetery with occasional or periodic clean-ups and grass cutting. These cemeteries can be found in the middle of cities and out in the country all over the United States.

16.1.2 Who to Contact When Checking on a Cemetery

Each state has a Cemetery Board, usually found at the state capitol. Some are well run and take an active part in the governing and enforcement of state cemetery laws. Others are poorly run, understaffed, and may be simply part of the local political gratuity system. A Cemetery Board should be able to inform you if they have had any complaints or have taken any action against any cemetery in the state. Periodically newspapers will have stories of cemeteries and misappropriation of maintenance funds.

You also can call your local Better Business Bureau. You will want to ask them if there have been any complaints filed with the bureau. If so, what has the bureau done as follow-up? While it seems you are wasting your time calling both the Board and Bureau to ask the same questions, it is possible that one has information while the other does not. This happens because upset consumers may think they need only to call one place and that one place will pass the information on. Not always. Bureaucracy can be slow and the information flow non-existent.

Consumers may not know about the state cemetery boards, or think cemeteries are not "businesses," and therefore the local Better Business Bureau is not an option. Cemeteries are businesses whether they are religious or not, for profit or not, or privately owned or not. All are businesses and consumers have a right to complain and see some kind of action taken.

16.2 What Options Are Available

16.2.1 Plot

A plot is a space in the ground. The most used and best known of cemetery products, the most traditional in the U.S. is the plot, and involves the burial of human remains. There are single, double and triple plots available at some cemeteries. These multi-plots can be one above another or side-by-side. They are not just one big space but are partitioned. They can be used all at the same time (two or three people die at the same time and are to be buried together) or one burial at a time. Often when the first person in a couple relationship dies the mate will arrange for the multi-plot while planning for the mate's funeral and burial.

16.2.2 Crypt

A crypt is a tomb above ground. Rulers and the wealthy throughout history have had whole rooms, indeed, whole buildings, built exclusively to entomb their bodily remains, which would be enclosed in individual vault-like tombs. In the U.S. wealthy families built "family crypts," and as each family member died they were added to the group. These crypts were either underground rooms or above ground rooms/buildings.

While this practice by the wealthy hasn't completely disappeared, the modern more democratic crypt has appeared. It is a burial space above ground usually of concrete with granite or marble facings, into specially constructed spaces. Think of built-in dresser drawers. The wall has to be extra deep. Buildings housing crypt rooms are called "mausoleums." Modern mausoleums are building "extra-large" crypts for the extra-large person and may be several stories tall.

Like the burial plot there are multiple crypts, also either side-by-side or one above another. For graveside services the casket is located atop the plot. For crypt-side services the crypt may be open or closed.

Crypts are becoming more popular for both consumers and the funeral industry. Consumers have options of whether to be buried under or above ground. The funeral industry is taking an ancient practice and applying modern marketing techniques as ground space is disappearing in some areas of the country.

16.2.3 Niche

A niche is a comparatively small space in a wall, above ground, for urns that hold cremated remains. This may be free standing or in a room called a "columbarium." Instead of full size crypts there are small spaces (about two feet by two feet).

At the turn of the 19th-20th century Japanese immigrants, mostly in Hawaii and California, brought their custom of cremation from Japan. Using traditional cemeteries, small freestanding niches were built upon burial plots. Today, these cemeteries are still used.

16.3 Cost

Plots can cost from a few dollars to several thousand dollars. The cost can be determined by where the plot is located; the premium location gets premium prices. A premium location is considered one near the cemetery roadway or walkway, has a beautiful view, or is perceived by the public to be "better" than other locations. Obviously, multi-plots or crypts, double or triple, will cost more. Plots in big cities will cost more than plots in small towns and rural areas.

Crypts start at a few thousand dollars and can go up to $50,000 or more. Crypts and niches also have premium locations — placement in the wall. Within a vertical stack of six or seven crypt levels, the second and third levels, commonly called the "heart" and "eye" levels are the most expensive. The spot just below the ceiling, often called "heavenly," is the cheapest. If the crypts or niches are in a mausoleum that has a designated area that can be used for services, or is simply perceived by the public to be "special," the closer to this area the crypt or niche the more expensive it will be.

Niches run from less than $100 to several hundred dollars. Plots, crypts and niches have maintenance costs. Plots have ground maintenance such as cutting the grass. Crypts and niches have wall/building upkeep. These fees may be collected up front as part of the initial cost, through a maintenance fee or local taxes.

16.4 Other Possible Mandatory Costs
Plot: There is a charge for excavation of the plot (usually called "opening and closing"), interment of remains (placing the remains in the grave) and completion of burial site (replacing earth and sod) in place. Monuments such as headstones for the grave will include two costs: the making of the monument and the placement at the grave itself. Veteran cemeteries are not included in this category. Many cemeteries have their own rules and regulations regarding what type and size of monument may be used.

Crypt: Opening and closing, entombment, engraving of a plaque.

Niche: Opening and closing of niche and engraving of a plaque.

In the United States all remains must be in some kind of container for transport. If the remains are to be placed in a cemetery they must be in a container. Containers for plots and crypts would be caskets which run from less than a hundred dollars for cardboard type to many thousands of dollars for caskets made of precious woods and/or metals. Urns for cremated remains can be simple cardboard boxes, whimsical vessels or one-of-a-kind artwork.

All services and goods, no matter how insignificant they may seem to you, are part of the final arrangement inventory kept by the professionals. This is what they sell along with their time and knowledge. Cemetery salespeople, even those cemeteries affiliated with a church, are usually employees who are paid by commission, the more they sell the more they earn. Some sales personnel use the title "grief counselor." Grief counseling training may range from none to extensive.

Sally's husband, Ed, died unexpectedly, and Sally and her two adult sons needed to arrange for his funeral. On the day of the funeral, after the church services, an insistent cemetery administrator who demanded payment met Sally and her two sons at the gravesite in the cemetery. A grief-stricken Sally almost became hysterical. She had paid the funeral provider several thousand dollars, so what did this strident man want?

Sally had not paid for the cemetery personnel, those who dug the grave and would be lowering the casket into the grave, and replacing the earth and sod. Clearly, this should not have happened. All were at fault here. Sally did not know what goods and services were used at funerals and was under great stress during the entire process. Was there some kind of miscommunication? Unethical business practice? Sloppiness? The funeral provider did not provide the information needed and the cemetery administrator could certainly have been more sensitive.

Another tradition that still continues is the buying of multiple individual plots, crypts or niches for whole families. Often parents buy the multiples when the children are young. Problems arise when the children are grown. They have their own families, they differ on how they want the final disposition of their remains, or they are living in another area, which could be at a great distance or even in another country.

16.5 Virtual Cemeteries

There are electronic online cemeteries. If you have no idea what an "electronic online" is then welcome to the age of the computer.

Virtual cemeteries allow memorial "electronic tombstones" with some sites offering simple listings of the dead to elaborate multimedia sites with high-end graphics, sound and video of the departed. Some are for fee, others are free. Some take a fee for the listing but allow the viewing for free. To participate, one would go to one of the sites, follow the sign process, and then be able to create text, add pictures and sound in creating a virtual memorial to a deceased person.

This is a new undertaking (no pun intended...honest!) as is most everything on the Internet, and is run by people not in the funeral industry or by industry people.

16.6 Monuments

The word "monument" can be used when discussing a tombstone, headstone, crypt or niche marker. Monuments can be simple flat markers at a military cemetery, a large room-size ornate crypt, or what are now being called "vanity" tombstones.

16.6.1 History

Memorialization (the use of monuments) in America has grown through several eras of influence. Originally rather austere, the Puritans of the 1600s wished for a simple form of headstone, containing a winged death head or skull, which stood as a warning to the living to prepare for the "Final Judgment."

In the mid-1700s a religious revival, "The Great Awakening," which stressed forgiveness and redemption of the soul, helped propel monuments towards more decoration with winged cherubs, crowns and sunbursts.

During the Romantic period of the 1800s, monumental trends reflected images that evoked powerful emotions.

Monuments increased in size and became suffused with feelings. Death releases powerful emotions and these were reflected by weeping willow trees; angels draping themselves over stones; lambs; dogs (for fidelity); and the use of the cross. Victorian memorials of 100 to 150 years ago were large, ornate works of art in stone, because stone was easy to obtain and hand labor was cheap.

Large memorials were also an indication of one's status in society, and many of the rich competed with one another over elaborate memorials that included room-size crypts modeled after the royal families of Europe. During the 1800s, monuments became status symbols with the wealthier emulating an earlier European age with Bible-related verse and artwork.

At the turn of the century, monumental trends reflected the economic downturn of the country in general, with its influx of poor immigrants. During the 1920s and through the end of World War II, monuments became much smaller, much simpler, with only a name and date in many cases. Mass produced memorials dominated the market, and many were ordered directly from the Sears Roebuck catalog.

The 20th century saw two catalysts change tombstones. The depression of the 1930s shrank tombstone size and artistic endeavors. But it was the invention of the power mower that changed tombstones from the upright position to the flat. The 20th century also saw the advent of cemeteries as businesses. Maintenance costs were cheaper and easier with the flat tombstone.

16.6.2 Vanity Tombstones

This is a trend that started in the 1980s with computers and automated sandblasters. Before the 1980s special-made grave markers were too expensive for anyone except the very wealthy. Epitaphs (the lettering on the monument) were paid for by the letter and the artwork had to be chiseled by hand. Expensive stuff!

And now they are coming back up, one could say. Technology is changing the tombstone, from the traditional rectangle with the traditional Bible verse into whatever a person can think up and create. A full-size granite Mercedes automobile, an elephant, slot machines, pigs, poker hands... you get the picture.

The most popular of this new trend is the photo tombstone. It's about $200 to have a photo cut into granite with chemicals, lasers or sandblasting. There is even a solar powered tombstone that allows lights to go on at night. Epitaphs are moving from Bible-inspired verse to funny one-liners such as:

"Once I wasn't, then I was, and now I ain't again."

Tombstone artisans have always been a part of the history. After all, it was a professional tombstone cutter, Charles Pageau, who in 1914, after watching children playing with sewing spools and pencils, designed Tinker Toys, the classic children's toy, and still one of the most popular today. Some tombstones are still created by hand, the one-at-a-time type, with beautiful insets of stained glass, steel, bronze or different colored granite.

Not all religious cemeteries are happy with this creative trend and many will have strict rules. Some cemeteries that have the flush tombstone because of power mowers are starting to provide sections for the creative and offbeat. If you are interested, either for yourself or another, and you have a particular cemetery you wish to use, make sure you check to see if vanity tombstones are allowed.

❦

"No Hits – No runs – No Heirs"
(Epitaph of a single lady)

— Solitude in Stone newsletter

Body Disposition

"As long as I look good in the box, who cares!"

— A young lady from Pennsylvania

Today there is a dizzying array of options for people to consider in the final disposition of their bodies. Old practices and new technology have added variety. Once a person dies there are five general categories of disposition options available in the United States. The first four cost money to execute, the last one does not.

- **Burial.** The body may be buried in a cemetery or private land, at sea, or entombed above ground.
- **Cremation.** The body may be cremated and the cremated remains can be in a cemetery, kept with a survivor, scattered on land, sea and air, or made into jewelry.
- **Mummification.** Mummification of the body is an ancient tradition from a foreign land that has been modernized a bit, yet keeping the exotic ambiance.
- **Cryonics.** This involves freezing the body or body parts to be defrosted years or centuries hence when medical technology has produced cures, a totally modern technological concept.
- **Body/Organ Donation.** This is also a relative newcomer on the scene. Prior to the 20th century, medical schools (without the consent of the family, much less the departed) often used bodies of poor people. Organ donation is a 20th century phenomenon reflecting advances in organ transplant surgery and medical research.

17.1 Burial

With 6,000 deaths a day in the U.S. the majority of the

bodies are buried. It is still the most traditional and popular disposition. Bodies may be buried in the ground, above ground and in the sea. A sea burial is not to be confused with the scattering of cremated remains on the sea.

Bodies may be buried in a cemetery that may be public or private. Depending on local laws, in some places in the U.S. bodies may be buried on private land that is not part of a cemetery. Normal house-sized lots are not big enough for private burial. If you are interested in finding out if your area/lot would allow private burial call your local Health Department.

The burial service is usually held after the funeral service, usually immediately afterwards. There are cemeteries that have accommodations for both the service and burial, but in many cases the service and burial can be at two different places. There can be a funeral cortège, the line of cars with the hearse holding the coffin at the head of the line, wending its way from funeral service to burial service. The local authorities usually require a police escort.

17.1.1 Questions & Answers
What products to consider for a land burial?
Plot or crypt, casket, casket interior and monument.

What services should be considered for a land burial?
Plot excavation, burial and maintenance.

Can anyone be buried at sea?
Due to environmental laws, civilians, generally speaking, are not allowed to be buried at sea. Military personnel and some political leaders may be allowed a sea burial.

Why is burial so popular?
- Religious-led tradition
- Often times survivors want to say "goodbye" and need the body in their presence
- Entombment, technically not a burial, still allows survivors attention to the deceased while still in bodily form

- After trauma or disease ravages, survivors may want to have the last view of the deceased to be less ravaged
- Survivors feel the deceased "has suffered enough" in dying and burial is perceived as a "putting to rest" the suffering

17.2 Cremation

This is a treasure trove of trivia to muse upon. Thirty four years ago cremation was used in only about 3% of deaths in the U.S. In fact, in many places there were no cremations. In recent years the cremation rate has gone up all over the U.S. with the Pacific states having cremation rates of over 40%. Hawaii is the biggest user of cremation and Washington DC the lowest use of cremation. The overall U.S. average is about 20%.

Some mortuaries have their own crematoriums on-site and the body does not need to be transported to the crematorium from the mortuary. If you are dealing with a professional intermediary, such as a funeral director who contracts with an outside crematory provider (used by the funeral home in which no ownership of that crematory is held by the funeral home), that professional should inspect the crematory several times a year and be completely familiar with the crematory and staff.

One may deal directly with a crematorium as well. As discussed earlier they tend to be cheaper than a full service mortuary because they have fewer services/products to offer.

17.2.1 Questions & Answers
What is cremation?

It is the process of reducing the human body to bone fragments and particles, not ashes, through the use of intense heat and flame at a crematorium. The layperson usually refers to "the ashes" when speaking of the cremated remains, while the industry uses the word "cremains."

What is the procedure?

After a person dies the body is brought to a mortuary/

crematorium with proper documentation. The body is cremated and the cremains are put into a small box-like container that is given to the person authorized to take possession. The average adult cremains will weigh about five pounds. This is the basic lawful procedure.

What can I do with the container?

Quite a few things actually. You can keep it just as it is or buy a fancier container called an "urn." These urns can be everything from whimsical to pieces of art and cost from less than a hundred dollars to thousands of dollars. People have been known to keep urns on television sets (the deceased loved watching TV), in bookcases (make ideal bookends), or stowed away on a boat (the deceased loved boats). The cremains can be buried in a grave or placed in a niche.

Can cremains be scattered?

Years ago scattering remains from an airplane over the deceased's hometown or favorite area was very popular. Now it is illegal in many areas. In recent years environmental laws have affected how states enact laws on where and how cremated remains may be scattered. Usually, cremains may not legally be scattered or dumped into fresh water or on public lands since the cremains are viewed as a contaminant. Private lands can be more accessible. For example, golf fans can arrange to have their cremains scattered over the fairways at Pebble Beach, a famous golf course south of San Francisco, California.

Many cemeteries have special areas specifically for the scattering of cremains such as a rose garden. The scattering itself can be done by the deceased's family or friends, or done by a professional for a fee.

There is also the tradition of scattering the cremains in the sea. Loved ones, friends and business associates take a boat out and scatter the cremains. The group may have some kind of ceremony, religious or not, often accompanied by food and beverage. It can be as simple or elaborate as wished.

In Hawaii, when the deceased was a person who loved the ocean, the tradition is for a gathering of outrigger canoes at sea with the loved ones boarding and lots of leis (flower garlands worn around the shoulders). Guitars and ukuleles are played, songs are sung, and the armada takes off from the shore heading to deeper blue waters. The canoes form a circle, offer a prayer and often a chant, an oli, is chanted and the leis are gently flung into the water. The cremains may be scattered upon the water or a diver will take them down into the depths of the water and release the cremains, which will float to the top and eventually mingle with the blossoms and greenery of the leis.

Again, the rules vary, state by state, on what can legally be done and what documents are needed. Coastal states have many businesses that cater to sea scattering. Remember, if you are contracting for sea scattering the cost is additional to the costs of cremation. Most sea scattering businesses are not part of the funeral industry but a separate entity.

There are three ways to approach the arrangement of sea scattering. When making final arrangements (either for oneself or another) and using a funeral provider, one can have the sea scattering included as part of the product and services contracted. Obviously, you will have to check to see if the funeral provider can provide this service. Another option is to make the arrangements yourself by calling a sea scattering business. The third option is to enroll in a memorial society that has sea scattering as an option.

May I still have a funeral with a viewing if I am opting for cremation?

Yes. Cremation would be done after the funeral, whenever and however the person making the arrangements wants. A casket does not have to be purchased for a viewing or funeral. However, the funeral provider has a right to charge a fee for the rental of a casket.

Why use cremation?
- Because of cultural, religious tradition.
- Environmentally friendly.
- Gives flexibility to survivors for transportation or relocation.
- Allows for final disposition at a time convenient for the family and loved ones.
- It seems the practical thing to do because of distance, logistics or finances.
- You want to.
- Being able to "give a piece of yourself" to others. Instead of loved ones being buried near one another, individuals want to parcel out their cremains to one or more people, places or type of dispersal, an increasingly common practice.

What's the cost?

The difference can be from less than five hundred dollars to several thousand dollars. Cost factors can be such things as transportation of the body, cremation container, cremation, professional staff and their services, paperwork with additional costs such as cremation urn, funeral services or the transfer of the cremains.

There are two approaches to cost in using cremation. One may use a crematorium directly and ask for the most basic arrangement that would include pick up of the body, cremation, completion of paperwork and one death certificate. This is the simplest and cheapest solution for a simple death. Any complications will add to the cost. Do note that some states require a container be used but there is no law that cannot allow one to use a cardboard container.

The full service mortuary may be more expensive. Why? When one goes to the Emergency Room at a hospital the bill can be very expensive, even for a relatively simple problem. This is because the hospital has high "overhead" costs — what it costs to operate the entire Emergency Room — and these costs are passed on to the customer. The same is true with a full-service mortuary. However, it also may depend on the neighborhood. The poorer the neighborhood the lower the price for goods and services, including mortuaries.

There are unique "extras" available. Terry Dieterle, an undertaker from Aurora, Illinois, offers his "Heirloom Pendant Collection" pieces, which come in yellow gold, white gold and diamonds. A small portion of cremains or a lock of hair from the departed can be permanently sealed inside the pendant. The cost of the pendants ranges from $1,900 to $10,000.

There is truly something for everyone and a price range for all budgets. All need to be checked out to see if the price and procedure is what you can afford and really want for yourself or others.

Who does one contact for a cremation?

One may telephone or visit any mortuary and inquire about their services and cost for cremation. If interested in using a crematorium directly one may ask a full-service mortuary for the name and phone number of a crematorium they could recommend, look in the yellow pages, or ask someone who has had to arrange for a cremation. Crematories and mortuaries have someone on call 24 hours a day.

Anything else available?

How about outer space? One enterprising organization is offering a "space burial." Actually it is a symbolic "burial" as only a few grams of the cremains are used in a lipstick sized capsule. A company in Houston, Texas buys capacity on commercial satellites and for about $5,000 a few grams of the deceased's cremains may orbit the earth for 18 months to ten years aboard a booster rocket. Eventually the booster rocket will fall back to earth, burning into nothing. This $5,000 doesn't include the actual cremation.

Another option is a sea scattering in a most spectacular way via fireworks. For about $2,200 a company in Los Angeles, California will take six people on a boat out to sea. The cremains have been packed into ten fireworks shells and are on a towboat. As arranged by the person or people responsible for the cremains the fireworks are shot off. As the shells burst the cremains are released into the fireworks display. The owners of the business have a background in professional fireworks displays, and had to procure five disparate California permits and licenses.

If you are breaking with familial tradition in deciding on cremation do make sure to talk this idea over with your family or loved ones. Put your wishes in writing. Contact and contract with your cremation provider. Even then it may be hard for the survivors to follow your wishes. Ruby J. had expressed her desire to her family to be cremated upon her death, breaking the family tradition of a Baptist burial. Ruby was killed in an automobile accident. The unexpectedness of the tragedy combined with the traditional Baptist grieving was too much for the family and they did not have Ruby's body cremated. A cousin commented later about the stress of not following Ruby's wishes combined with the tremendous grief of her death.

"We were trying to get through the days... it was horrible. Was the funeral for us or for Ruby? I don't know. We didn't get to say 'goodbye' to Ruby. In fact, we didn't get to see her. There couldn't be a viewing because she got hit pretty hard in the accident. I don't know... it felt comforting standing at her grave, knowing her body was there... not just a bunch of ashes..."

17.3 Mummification

Mummification is a process for preservation of the body. Up until 400 A.D., people of different religious sects practiced mummification of the dead body. The Egyptians were considered the masters at this technique that was a dehydration process, extracting the body fluids. Most famous of these are the ancient royal rulers of Egypt. Today in the U.S. it might be possible to include mummification in your final arrangements. There is one company that is affiliated with the funeral industry that can legally offer this arrangement.

The name of the non-profit organization is "Summum" and it is located in Salt Lake City, Utah (see "Resources"). They state they are the only mummification business in the world and can send you a free brochure.

The ancient Egyptians used a dehydration process, removing the body fluids. Today the process is different from the ancient Egyptians in that it is a wet, chemical process with the body immersed in chemical preservatives. The mummified body is placed into a mumiform, which is an airtight container. It is shaped like a human body with a "life mask" of the person on the outside, reminiscent of the ancient Egyptian containers. It is transported in an air tray on the airplane to the mortuary that has contracted the service.

17.3.1 Questions & Answers

How did this come about?

A business of making sacramental wine in a pyramid shaped building in Salt Lake City, Utah, got lots of comments about mummification and people starting coming forward saying they were interested in being mummified when they died. A non-profit organization was created and has been incorporated in Salt Lake City since 1975.

The founder, Claude Nowell, owner of the wine business, who eventually changed his name to Corky Ra, became interested in the process. He met John Chew, Director of Funeral Service Education and Anatomy at Lynn University, in Boca Raton, Florida. It took several years to perfect the process.

How do I make arrangements?

Call Summum and ask for their free brochure. If you have additional questions ask them. They also have a Web (Internet) site. Contact your funeral director/mortuary, as a licensed funeral director must make this arrangement because the remains need to be transported out of state. They will make the arrangements for the body to be transported to and from Florida, the site of the process.

What if my funeral director hasn't heard of this?

Summum is listed in the Yellow Book (your funeral director knows of this book) under "mummification." If you are looking for a funeral provider this may be a consideration for you — does the funeral provider have any experience with clients wishing to use mummification?

How long does it take?

Including transportation it can be from 30 to 60 days, depending on the condition of the body.

How much does it cost?

The mummification process itself is several thousand dollars. That does not include any other expenses. According to Summum, most clients who have pre-arranged their own mummification upon their death take out life insurance policies to pay for the entire funeral process, including the mummification.

Can my mummified remains be buried?

Decomposition of the remains happens if the remains are unprotected against ground contamination such as water or pollutants. A special vault that is sealed would have to be used. Summum recommends an above-the-ground disposition such as a mausoleum. No, the mumiform cannot be stored in your house. Cremains may be stored in a private home but not human bodies, even if they are mummified.

Can people take a peek at the mummified remains?

To take a peek would start deterioration. That is why the mumiform is sealed.

May I still have a funeral?

Yes, before or after the mummification. Before the mummification it would be possible, under certain circumstances to have a funeral with a viewing. After the mummi-fication there could be no viewing but there could be funeral services with the mumiform instead of the casket. If you are interested in religious rites such as a church funeral, do confirm with your church that mummification is allowed in that religion's doctrine.

What does a mummy look like?

Wrapped in linens, the body looks like a sleeping person.

17.4 Cryonics

This is for people who want to pop up again in the future. If you are going to die due to organ failure or disease, you can be frozen, what in cryo-speak is called *cryonic suspension*, and hopefully revived later when whatever ails you has had a cure or replacement discovered. At this point it is "hopefully" because no human has been revived to date. The movie "Aliens" showed the space crew in suspension for many years as the space ship traveled to a far off planet. Unlike reality, the actors "awoke" no worse for their long sleep.

Cryonics first started in the United States in 1964 when introduced via a book, "The Prospect of Immortality," and the first body actually placed in suspension (kind of a high-tech freeze) was in 1967. That body is still in suspension. The legality of cryonics was taken to court in California and successfully became legal under the "anatomical gift act" which was used as the basis for uniformity. Technically there is no national law regarding cryonics but it has never been declared illegal in any state.

However, there are instances where a person's wish can be over-ridden such as in Wisconsin where the spouse can override the dead spouse's wishes, including having cryonic suspension. The opposite has also happened. The next-of-kin of a dead person wanted the dead person to undergo cryonic suspension. While the paperwork was in process someone found a note that had been written by the deceased some time prior to the death and the deceased mentioned that cryonic suspension was not wanted. The cryonic organization immediately withdrew from the request.

The procedure entails the body's blood being replaced with an anti-freeze solution and liquid nitrogen. The body is then wrapped in tinfoil, put into a polyethylene bag, and lowered into a capsule filled with liquid nitrogen.

17.4.1 Questions & Answers

How much does it cost?

The cost can go from $28,000 to $150,000, depending on where the contract is made. At this time there are cryonic businesses in Michigan (Cryonic Institute), Arizona (Alcor Life Extension Foundation) and California (CryoCare in Los Angeles, Trans Time, Inc. in Oakland). Canadians will find a Cryonic Society in Toronto. Two non-profit organizations are the International Cryonics Foundation in Stockton, California and the American Cryonics Society in Santa Clara, California.

Funding is usually done by life insurance policies. Part of the funds goes to paying the membership fee, the initial cost of getting the body to suspension, and the rest of it is invested and goes for the ongoing cost of maintenance.

How does one know if the cryonic organization is legitimate?

Check to see how long the organization has been in business. You should be able to go see the place where people are in suspension. Call your state's Attorney General and Better Business Bureau to see if any complaints have been filed. There should be some kind of board of directors and you should be able to go to a board meeting as a guest.

What's the difference between the non-profit and for-profit?

For investors the non-profit investment provides a tax deduction while the for-profit investment is to make money. The for-profit investment is still theoretical, as the cryonics businesses are not making a profit as yet. The non-profit organizations take legal custody of the body for maintenance and operate storage and maintenance facilities. The for-profit businesses do the actual cryonic procedure and their facilities are contracted by the non-profit organizations.

Do I have to freeze my whole body?

No. It can be the whole body or a piece of it such as the brain.

What kind of people are performing the cryonic procedure?

The technical staff is science-oriented with people who have Ph.D.'s in such areas as physiology, biochemistry or biophysics. The people in cryonics tend to be well-educated, rational people with a scientific interest.

There is also cryonics humor such as the cryonics song, "For he's ['freeze'] a jolly good fellow!", the cryonics motto, "Never say die!" and the cryonics band, "The Ungrateful Dead".

17.5 Body/Organ Donation

Many people do not do body/organ donations. Only 1% consider donation or the survivors agree to donation. A body donation is an arrangement that is set up prior to the actual death. Body donation is for medical school use. Generally speaking, the organization that coordinates such donations will also be in charge of transportation and basic paper work such as the death certificate. The donor, after filling out forms that declare their intention of donating their body to a designated medical school is given a phone number survivors will call upon the donor's death.

An organ donation, which may be set up ahead of time by the donor or consented to by the survivors after death, must be completed in a short time span. After death the organs shut down very fast; therefore the organs need to be harvested within minutes or hours. Many donors have an organ donor stamp on their driver's license but that will not guarantee the donation will happen upon the donor's death.

17.5.1 Questions & Answers

How do I find a body donation organization?

One of the requirements for body donation is the proximity of the death to the medical school for which it is intended. Therefore the search will be in your local area. The best way is to call your local medical school and ask about body donation if you wish to consider it for yourself upon your death. An authorized agent of the deceased can give consent in a hospital as they have the facilities to keep the body until transport.

For any other facility or home/public death the agent may or may not be successful unless pre-planned due to logistics and legal procedures.

What kind of organs can be donated?

Medical technology has made it possible for just about everything human to be harvested and used in a transplant such as corneas (eyes), heart, lungs, bone and skin, just to name a few.

How does one go about donating organs?

If set up ahead of time (may be part of a Medical Directive packet) the donor will have an organ donor card to keep. If the donor has a driver's license the Motor Vehicle Department can generate an organ donor driver's license. If not pre-planned, many hospitals will have someone contact the survivors after the death to ask if organ donation is an option.

Does body/organ donation cost anything?

No. With body donation there is not always a choice of body disposition. An ethical organization will be able to explain exactly what form of body disposition they use or if the survivors will be able to retrieve the body. Most use cremation. This means there is no cost born by the deceased's survivors. With organ donation, once the organs are harvested the authorized agent who will be responsible for body disposition legally owns the deceased's remains.

A Basic Check List Of What Needs To Be Done Following A Death

"La muerte no necesita razones."
(Death needs no excuses.)

— Traditional Mexican/Southwest saying

When someone dies, exactly what does need to be done? Literally. Even if some pre-planning has been done, an individual or group of people will need to do a variety of tasks. People may be emotional, confused and the situation may be foreign to all involved. Under these circumstances figuring out what to do may be difficult.

This is a generic checklist. Much depends on personal preferences, religion and circumstances of death. This checklist is for after death happens. It is in a general chronological order but each situation is different. You may not need everything listed; there may be tasks you need to do that are not on this list. Information relating to these different tasks will be found in appropriate chapters.

✔ Decide on body disposition if not already planned
✔ If using body/organ donation
    - *Not pre-arranged:* inform medical personnel
    - *Pre-arranged:* call phone number provided
✔ Contact provider, if using professionals
✔ What services/products wanted, fees, how to pay
✔ Documents
    - *Death Certificate:* how many needed
    - *Transit Permit/Cremation Permit:* procurement
    - *Authorized Agent:* have available if needed

✔ Transportation of body

✔ Rituals with body such as a special washing or clothing

✔ Deceased employed: contact employer

✔ Deceased self-employed: contact whomever working with / for / project

✔ Deceased a minor/student: contact school

✔ Deceased retired: contact Social Security, pension, Medicare

✔ Arrange wake / viewing / funeral / memorial service / body disposition

> *Wake:* location with directions, date and time
>
> *Viewing:* location with directions, date(s) and time
>
> *Funeral / memorial service:* location with directions, date and time. If people are traveling from a great distance, allow enough time
>
> *Body disposition such as burial services, cremated remains scattered, etc.:* location with directions, date and time, additional information needed

✔ Contact those people who would be invited to the above

✔ If no funeral, body disposition service, need to inform everyone connected with deceased on deceased's death. This can be done by:

> *Phone call:* use deceased's phone book, papers, and neighbors
>
> *Mail:* a letter, card, announcement (gaining popularity are do-it-yourself postcards with a picture of the deceased included.)

✔ Designate someone to be the host/co-coordinator of funeral, memorial, disposition

✔ Obituary: contact newspaper(s), provide following information:

Hometown and current town of deceased, date of birth and death, marriage date(s), names of family, personal and professional endeavors, cause of death (optional), funeral and memorial service(s), picture of deceased (ask if wanted). Obit writer can write the actual copy but they would appreciate the information written/printed out neatly and cleanly on plain paper. Faxing is quick and convenient. *(Note: there can be a fee for the obituary)*

✔ Plan and collect deceased's outfit for burial or cremation: clothing, jewelry, personal mementos

✔ Plan future memorial service(s): location, date and time

Arrange for someone to co-ordinate each future memorial service

Contact other people / institutions regarding death / memorial service

✔ Contact deceased's lawyer

✔ Authorized Agent settle bank accounts, close out bills, stop services/products

✔ Thank you notes sent as needed

"Billy, whose wife Effie was no good and would never take care of Billy, was suitably buried after he died in Idaho. He was first to die. Ray went up and brought his body back. Ray was next to die. Mama followed and she got the curb that she wanted. Sister died next and got the grave on the left because she was left-handed. The next death was my husband Matt. The funeral home called me to ask which grave I wanted opened for him so I said the 'middle' without giving it much thought. Later a friend, Jean, was buried in the fifth grave. Now, when I go, I will be buried in the last grave. And there will be Matt with Jean on one side and me on the other."

— *I Never Rode A Camel Across The Desert*
by Virginia McLeod

PART IV
DEATH ETIQUETTE

And then there was the widow who, less than three months after her husband's death, married his brother. She hung a large picture of her late husband in the living room, hoping thereby to soften criticisms of her hasty remarriage.

One day a visitor asked, "Who is that handsome man in the photograph?" And she was ready for the question.

"Oh," she answered with a proper note of sadness in her voice, "that was my poor brother-in-law. He died recently."

— American Funeral Director Magazine

My Condolences...

"Oh, geez! Oops, sorry...geez...uh, I....oh, geez!"

— Teenager at first memorial service,
who accidentally tipped over urn,
picture of deceased and two pots of flowers

What does one say or write to survivors of the deceased? It is a social obligation that has little, if any, resources. Personal and business obligations may mean going to a funeral of someone you don't really know. Not knowing what to say to the survivors, you may opt to stay away from them. This chapter gives suggestions for various situations.

The commercial condolence card business is booming. With a nice little generic verse a person only need sign a name and the social obligation is done. However, a personal note can give a mourner a lift, even if only for a moment.

Another area of death etiquette is the funeral. Individuals today often will be going to a funeral for someone who is of another religion or of another culture. As a visitor one will want to have some basic information relating to the deceased's religion or culture as it relates to death and the particular funeral process. What to do, say, wear or bring will help a visitor relax and not be afraid of accidentally offending others.

19.1 People Responsible for Funeral/Memorial Arrangements

- In these times of divorce there are a lot of "ex" people around. Do invite "ex's" to the funeral or memorial service. The "ex" is there to pay respects, not bring up old arguments or grievances.

- Do write "thank-you" notes! Thank people who gave flowers, donated to a fund in the deceased's name, brought things or helped out. You may want someone (a friend or relative) to help you do this as it can be exhausting.

- Do have a notice in the newspaper whenever possible and telephone people whom you want to know of the death. If funeral arrangements are pending make sure someone, if not yourself, is available to take telephone calls and is able to answer questions regarding funeral/memorial services. If people are arriving from out-of-town they may need help with directions, transportation and lodging.

- Do appoint someone, if you are unable, to "host" funeral/memorial service to be able to greet guests, oversee the service and attend to any problems.

19.2 Do's and Don'ts Regarding a Death

- Don't go to a funeral or memorial service unless you know you are invited or you know it is open to the public.

- If you don't know how the deceased died don't ask the family at the funeral.

- Respect same-gender partners who are grieving. No matter what your personal beliefs are regarding homosexuality, a same-gender partner is grieving over a loved one's death. Don't give your opinion. Do acknowledge all survivors and don't take sides.

- If the death is a result of suicide do not ask why the suicide was committed. If there is no funeral do not suggest to the mourners they should have one. The survivors usually are going through feelings of shock, surprise, anger and guilt. There may be reactions such as, "How come I didn't pick up on something like that?" There may be self-blame to the point of acute emotional or even physical distress. There can be conflicts amongst the survivors. A hand written note with condolences would be appreciated. Simply writing "You are in my thoughts at this difficult time" can suffice.

- Regarding the death of a child. If you yourself are a bereaved parent, if you have experienced the death of your own child, you are able to tell the grieving parents that you know how they feel and that you understand, if you wish to do so. But if you are not a bereaved parent, do not attempt to empathize with them by telling them that you know how they feel. That can be perceived as insincere.

19.3 What to Say or Write Regarding a Death

"Please accept my sympathy for your recent tragedy."

This is a good generic thing to say or write to people who are mourning the loss of someone who was young or died unexpectedly.

"Please accept my sympathy for your recent loss."

These examples are slightly different. In the latter, the loss may not necessarily have been a tragedy (an elderly person, for example, who dies not of an accident or homicide). It is not necessarily a tragedy when an elder dies (of natural causes, including disease and illness) for that is what happens in the cycle of life. Your sympathy is not that it is a tragedy that the person died, but the fact that the survivors are grieving the loss of that person being in their lives. It is possible that if the deceased had a long and maybe painful dying, death often becomes a relief, for both the deceased and the survivors. That doesn't necessarily make the loss any less.

Both of the above examples may be used with people you know or with strangers. There may be circumstances of attending a funeral, or having to send a card to strangers. When either the deceased or the survivors are strangers, or if you do not know how the deceased died, the latter expression of sympathy would be more prudent.

"I am so sorry for your loss."

This is a simple but heartfelt thing to say or write when the deceased is a child or a young person. If you knew the child, and you can honestly say or write some nice things about the child, it would be appropriate to do so. However, if you do not know the child, keep to something simple like the above example.

With so many people working today it is possible a co-worker will die and you need to send a note of condolence. Write about your relationship with the deceased at work, something you shared or did. Anything. These notes, no matter how mundane the activity or thoughts will give the mourner(s) great comfort. The contents of the note will be a brief break for the mourner from the sadness and loss. It is quite possible the mourner will treasure those notes for many years.

The above suggestions are just that...suggestions. If you feel tongue-tied or awkward, these suggestions give you simple but effective ideas of what to say or what to write.

Traditionally, Americans associate the color black with death and funerals. But that is changing and one will see many colors. For many groups black is not the color to wear. In fact, now the color black is used at weddings! Times change...so do the "proper" colors.

Euthanasia

*"How do you end your own life
with certainty and grace?"*

— Derek Humpfry,
author, *Final Exit*

The word "euthanasia," from the Greek "eu" meaning "well" and "thanatos" meaning "death" has come to mean the act or method of causing death painlessly, so as to end suffering. In the United States euthanasia has a history of use with animals. Farmers, hunters, veterinarians, animal owners, all have had to "put down" injured and sick animals.

Human euthanasia has had a shorter, much more controversial history in the United States. In 1938 a Unitarian minister, Reverend Charles Potter, founded the first American euthanasia organization devoted to the premise of allowing humans the right, under certain circumstances, to die.

Other organizations were founded but the debate did not become very public until the case of Karen Ann Quinlan. In a coma for eight years, her parents wanted the mechanisms that kept her alive disconnected. Requiring years of legal wrangling, the parents finally won the case in 1976.

A point of contention from this case was the fact that the parents were asking for the disconnection, not Karen herself. The idea of having some kind of document that would tell the medical profession (and others) what an individual wanted in regards to one's own death took hold and the first Living Will was created in California.

The debate between "passive" and "active" euthanasia surfaced. Passive means no medical intervention in the process of dying. When a person is being kept alive through a life support system (i.e. feeding or breathing tube) either the dying person or a designated other person can have this support system turned off. A person may require so much pain medication that it hastens death. Both of these situations are called "passive euthanasia" and are practiced throughout the United States.

Active euthanasia is intervention that hastens an inevitable death such as physician-aided suicide, also known as physician aided death. Although there are physicians who help a patient die, active euthanasia did not become public until Dr. Jack Kevorkian, a pathologist in Michigan, helped a woman die on June 4, 1990. Hailed and assailed he continued to help people die even as he was brought to trial on more than one occasion. He is currently serving a life sentence in prison.

The same year, 1990, another famous medical case that ended up in the Missouri court system allowed for the disconnection of the feeding tube for Nancy Cruzan, also in a coma. Upon the heels of this case the United States Supreme Court recognized the right for a patient to refuse medical treatment or be voluntarily removed from life-support equipment. The Natural Death Act, which allows for the removal of life sustaining mechanisms, was enacted.

Today, Oregon is the only state with legal euthanasia. Other states are debating the issues. While illegal in all states but Oregon, the reality is that euthanasia may or may not be part of people's lives and deaths.

A dying person or designated person may have to make the decision on passive euthanasia. It may be made after a consensus with other family members, or without family members' support. Therefore, in addition to mourning the loss of the deceased there may also be guilt and/or anger amongst the survivors.

This situation creates potential difficulties for the survivors. You may or may not know if this circumstance applies. Whatever your opinions on euthanasia, when sending a condolence card, paying your respects, or attending a funeral or memorial service, it is not for you to inquire, argue or debate the issue.

Ricardo was diagnosed with a terminal disease and as the pain and physical disability became intolerable to him, he and his wife talked about euthanasia. He wanted to die but his religion forbade it, and they knew their grown kids wouldn't approve. After several months of suffering and talking to one another, Ricardo planned and executed his own death with pills he had collected over the months.

His wife, filled with grief and sadness and feeling so alone, told her adult children how their father had died. Feeling very angry two of the siblings didn't attend the funeral, and the other two attended the funeral. However, one never spoke to her mother and the other sibling became so agitated she had to leave the funeral. A neighbor of the husband and wife took it upon herself to lambaste the wife for being "...a terrible wife..." in front of all the guests at the funeral.

With this complex issue, it may be the case that the family is against euthanasia but the deceased was for it, and the family is grieving both the loss of the deceased and the way the deceased chose to die. The opposite is also true with the family supportive of the deceased's wishes. They may or may not wish to share these feelings with others.

This privacy must be respected. Mourning the dead and grieving with the survivors is not the time to debate issues. "Paying one's respects" and supporting those who are mourning the loss is a social obligation whether to strangers or loved ones, not a debate forum.

What does one say or write as condolence in this type of situation? If you are invited to a final gathering, whether you know it is a final gathering or not, you can grieve for the loss of the deceased and you can share your knowledge of the deceased. This is particularly true of a note.

This contentious debate is far from over and people become very emotional on both sides. This has an impact on dying people's wishes and those grieving and the complexity of the situation is even greater. These two groups, the dying and the mourning, are often targets of debate, and most ironically, it is these two groups who are the most vulnerable.

Funeral Practices
Of Different Cultures
In The United States

"Aum Nama Sivaya"

— Hindu mantra for
victim of sudden death

Today it is estimated there are about 140 different languages spoken in the United States and about 35-40 million Americans whose preferred language is not English. This is America's history, people emigrate from different countries and bring their cultures and religions with them to add to the cultures already here, creating a country of religious diversity and cultural heritage.

It is most likely that one may be invited to a funeral or memorial for someone who was of another culture or religion. What does one do? Bring? Say? Here are some general, brief descriptions of cultural views and religious beliefs around the end of life.

21.1 Native American

There are over 350 different tribes in the United States and each has its own customs and traditions for death. This book cannot attempt to discuss all tribes, as this would require hundreds of pages. This chapter is not a scholarly tome on Native American death customs, but more of a general guide for the uninitiated. Some customs will be listed here. If you are invited to a funeral service and have any questions regarding death etiquette ask the person who invited you to the funeral. They will be able to answer your questions or refer you to someone who can. The fact that you recognize the fact there can be traditions and customs you may not be familiar with demonstrates your ability to honor the difference.

Many tribes believe in chanting certain death chants at the time of death, particularly for a loved one. Dying alone is not considered to be a positive situation in general.

Wakes are common and the gathering can be quite large. If held at the funeral home, access will be around the clock. There may be a prescribed number of days the body lies in state. If the funeral home cannot accommodate the large crowd, the wake may also be held at a school, church or community hall. Food is common.

Many tribes have family members wash and prepare the body for burial. Embalming is not always performed. If the individual is Catholic a priest may say Mass. The family may also request traditional Native American ceremonies that involve a medicine man or singer. The Navajo of the southwest are a good example. The body is removed from the location where the death occurred whether it is a hospital or hogan (home), and made ready for burial that should occur as soon as possible.

There are tribes that have the tradition of putting some of the deceased's belongings in the casket with the deceased. A fine saddle has been known to rest upon the casket.

In the Native American traditions, bodies are not always put into a casket, which is considered a Christian missionary influence. Corpses can be shrouded or wrapped in a special blanket. A beautiful melding of the two traditions is found with the contemporary Osage of Oklahoma. Each family arrives with a burial blanket, two feet by three feet, handmade, and each male puts his blanket on the casket. At the end of the funeral service the men line up and take a blanket. If it looks like a man will get his own blanket back, he will step out of line, and back in so he won't get his own back. These blankets are only used for funerals.

Some tribes have funeral traditions that strike some observers as overly simple or austere. This may be because the tribe views death as a natural process, such as the Apache, so the process of mourning and grieving is limited. In contrast, family and friends in the Navajo tribe do not want to participate in the funeral because of beliefs about ghosts. Whether the tribal member actually believes in ghosts, especially the younger and more educated, is not what perpetuates this custom. It is part of that tribal tradition.

On the other hand the Plains tribes such as the Cree, Crow, Blackfoot, Cheyenne and Kiowa may express sorrow more openly, coming from an old tradition of appeasing the Gods in order to spare the living.

There are tribes that have the custom of assisting in filling in the grave at graveside ceremonies. If a visitor is given a possession of the dead person after the burial, consider it a great honor. Do accept the possession with grace and thanks.

21.2 Asian Examples

There are dozens of Asian groups in the United States and a whole book could be written about these groups alone. The following is intended to briefly describe three representative groups in the United States. The U.S. is home to Asian Americans who have been in the United States for generations as well as recent immigrants. They may or may not still practice some of the homeland traditions or possibly be part of a mainstream religion in the U.S, and don't practice any of the "old" traditions.

21.1.1 Japanese - cremation is preferred and the funeral service could be a Memorial service with pictures of the deceased. The Japanese prayer, Makura or Kyo, ("pillow prayer" or "bedside prayer") is a tradition in Japanese-American families as well as Japanese immigrants, that the family will recite. It is traditional to serve food at the funeral home itself, which is equipped with a kitchen in many areas. Otherwise the food will be served someplace else.

21.1.2 Chinese - traditionally Chinese preferred burial to cremation as the bones needed to be in the ground and the gravesite was a focus of ancestral ritual. In earlier days, and still seen in Hong Kong and Taiwan, the deceased's bones would be kept in a special pot, to be returned to the "motherland" — mainland China. This is no longer done in the United States. Ceremonies can include Taoist, Buddhist, Confucian, Christian or Muslim components.

21.1.3 Vietnamese - prefer burial and may have an elaborate funeral and burial procession with Catholic or Buddhist rituals. Incense and votive papers are burned.

21.3 Black/African-American

In Africa one religion is the Yoruba in Nigeria. Like Christianity there are different sects with differing traditions for the disposal of the deceased that include reincarnation, vultures, cremation and burial. There can be an altar in the home with items belonging to the deceased. On the deceased's birthday favorite foods of the dead one are put around the altar in order that he or she will have the essence of the food. Expensive perfumes and oils are also placed about the alter. The Yoruba are considered "earth people" with life and continuity coming from the earth. Colonized Africa brought the Catholic religion that introduced the worship of saints. The Africans renamed Catholic saints such as St. Michael to an African name of *Shango*.

It was against this backdrop that African males and females were enslaved and sent to America (and elsewhere). As slaves they were not allowed to practice their religious beliefs, at least in public. Over the centuries in the United States other religions were introduced into the black culture. Today, like other racial groups, there is no monolithic single religion practiced by Black-Americans; however, it is not uncommon at black funerals today to find threads of another time and place.

The gathering of friends and family for the funeral and burial are very important. The body of the deceased might remain unburied for a period of up to several weeks allowing distant family members to arrive for the funeral and for money to be procured to pay for the funeral. Pre-pay planning as well as organ donation is not common in the black community. The body may be moved to different places for more than one service before actual burial. Occasionally in rural areas the body is "laid out" in the home and a wake is held there.

Singing, particularly of hymns, is prevalent at the funeral. Cremation is not usually considered except when there is financial distress. "Home-going" or "tribute to life" are phrases that are often used to describe the funeral service. "Funeral Programs" with the deceased's picture and obituary are handed out before the service. Pageantry and display are common.

In black churches, if communion is part of the service, it could either be served just to the family, who is taking communion for the deceased, or for the entire congregation. Don't wear red to the funeral. A more subdued color such as white, black or gray is considered good etiquette. The minister may use very expensive oils particular to death rituals such as anointing the casket and/or vault for safekeeping.

Pallbearers are usually family or close friends. Open casket funerals are common and often the face of the deceased is covered with a fine cotton, linen or silk shroud just prior to the closing of the casket, the deceased is "never in darkness." Flowers, particularly floral arrangements are common. Be careful about what kind of arrangement you send. For example, if you are not a close friend or family it would not be appropriate to send a heart-shaped arrangement. The family would consider that offensive. If in doubt about the floral arrangement a basket is always proper. The family will always pay for the casket floral arrangement. Unless specifically asked, do not offer to help pay for the casket arrangement.

The status the deceased had in the community is important and the number of floral arrangements is considered an indication of this status. Other "indicators" are; how long the funeral procession to the gravesite is and if the children of the deceased all have new clothes. Large fraternal organizations will have their own traditions at the graveside. Flowers from the arrangements at the gravesite are often taken for pressing in the family Bible.

It is appropriate to take flowers and food (repast) to the home of the deceased. In place of cut flowers a fruit tree (if the deceased's family lives in a house with a yard), or a potted plant (for apartment dwellers) is often given. To many, a cut flower represents death, while a tree or plant represents a re-establishment of life within the family. The deceased's spirit will inhabit the tree or plant, giving comfort to those grieving — "As this tree (or plant) lives so may the spirit of your loved one" — and the family will plant it immediately.

21.4 Hispanic

Hispanic (Spanish/Portuguese speaking) cultures includes much of the U.S., particularly the Southwest, Mexico, Central and South American, many Caribbean islands, Spain and Portugal.

Mexican (or Mexican-American) funerals may be strictly Roman Catholic while other Hispanic groups may have a combination of Catholic and indigenous traditions which remain and include various deities. In recent years Protestant influence is becoming observed, as well as the evangelical influence such as the Jehovah's Witness and Mormon.

Sometimes candles are used with varying meanings. Some people are healers and bring special death candles. For the viewing/ rosary guitars and music are often played. A visitor does not have to participate in the music, the healer's rituals, or bring candles. You may pay your respects to the deceased by stepping up to the open casket for a moment, if you wish, during the viewing before the funeral Mass.

It is quite common for the family to wash and prepare the body. The bathing of the body is a ritual and special liquids may be used. The idea is that it is supposed to clean every spirit the deceased possessed prior to death. This is not done in public but when the body arrives at the mortuary. The mortuary will allow the family to prepare the body for the viewing, rosary or Mass. As part of a tradition it does help the mourners start to work through their bereavement.

A Hispanic tradition that has carried over into the United States is the carrying of the casket on the shoulders of the pallbearers rather than holding onto the casket with handles.

The time to pay one's respects to the family is normally after the funeral mass and/or graveside service. Bringing flowers is always appropriate. Small bouquets or a small arrangement is traditional. It may be brought at any time, during the viewing, rosary, Mass or graveside service. If the mourning family is not affluent there may be a donation box or one may bring an envelope with cash. Cash is preferred in this situation.

21.5 Polynesian

Hawaiian, Samoan, Tahitian and Maori are some of the Polynesian groups originating from islands in the Pacific Ocean. Special flowers and leis may be used for the funeral service as well as draped on the casket. While each Polynesian group has its own culture, generally Polynesians prefer burial to cremation. The bones of the dead that carry the essence of the spirit are returned to the land, although cremation is also done. The sea, leis and mourners on boats are some of the customs.

Song and Polynesian dance during the funeral may be performed, often extemporaneously. Grief can be very demonstrative. A Polynesian style wake will include large amounts of food and drink. Monetary gifts (cash in a card) have become common. This is to help the family pay for all the food that is needed and any other debt incurred.

Polynesians are a demonstrative people with lots of touching and hugging, particularly at funerals. Kissing, the formal type, by both men and women is often done twice, once on each cheek.

Often, whatever religion the family practices is combined with some Polynesian rituals at funerals.

⚜

In Hawai'i the Plumeria flower is called the "make (ma-kay) man flower" which means the "dead man's flower" as the tree grows near cemeteries. The nickname doesn't stop the flower of being one of the most popular lei blossoms.

Different Funeral Customs
Of Religions In
The United States

*"Every soul shall have a taste of death. In the end to us
shall you be brought back"*

— Quran 29:57
Islamic holy book

22.1 Buddhist

Basic Buddhist theory suggests the most effective method of conquering dying is to accept death as the chief fact of life and as the main signal that all the things one hopes for will be utterly destroyed in due course, and that once one is able to neither long for or fear death, one is beginning to transcend both life and death and coming into unity with the "Changeless Absolute."

Buddhists come from several Asian countries with diverse ancient traditions and many recent converts in the United States. Quite often, due to acculturation, if a practice is handed down in the family, the younger generations don't always know the traditional rituals.

During the moment of death certain sutras (recorded teachings attributed to the Buddha) are chanted. Prayers or rituals may take place for a certain number of days following death. Both cremation and burial are practiced; however, cremation is usually preferred.

If death occurs while another Buddhist is with the deceased certain chants may be uttered. There is usually an open casket funeral with a monk, surrounded by burning incense, leading the mourners in a series of chants interwoven with the ringing of a gong. Non-Buddhists are not expected to know or participate in the chants. In one tradition, a special meal of rice, peas and carrots is prepared at the funeral home and taken to the crematorium (if not on the mortuary

premises), and whenever possible, the mourners walk to the crematorium, and there the monk will lead a thirty minute committal service.

22.2 Roman Catholic

A traditional funeral will include a vigil the night before the
funeral that can be held at the church or mortuary. A priest will conduct a rosary (responsive prayer and intercession to the Blessed
Virgin) and at the conclusion of the rosary the viewing will proceed.
If a visitor wishes to pay respects to the deceased, plan on doing so
at the viewing. For the funeral Mass the casket will be closed. The
vigil will commence at a given time. Non-Catholics are not expected to participate in the rosary itself, and viewing the deceased is
entirely a personal choice.

The day following the formal Catholic church service, the funeral Mass is held at the designated church. It lasts about 40 minutes.
Non-Catholic visitors do not have to participate in the kneeling or
communion but may simply sit in the pew. At a certain point in the
funeral Mass the priest may ask everyone to stand for a reading or
for prayers, or invite participants to greet one another with a sign
(handshake, hug, kiss) of peace.

The conclusion of the Roman Catholic funeral consists of the
rite of committal at the graveside. The priest will offer graveside
prayers and then sprinkle holy water upon the grave and casket.
Placing a flower on the casket or taking flowers home is customary.
Quite often the mortician will pull a few flowers from the casket
spray and give them to the bereaved. Mourners are not expected to
stay for the actual burial.

A characteristic of the Roman Catholic funeral is the giving
of a Mass card to the family. Non-Catholics are welcome to participate in this way. A Mass card with envelope may be picked up at any
Roman Catholic church. During the daily Mass there is a section for
praying for the deceased. For a small fee a priest will offer a Mass for
the name of the person listed on the card. At the funeral Mass there
will be a "guest book," usually on a pedestal, where one may sign

their name. The Mass card may be left there, mailed to the bereaved, or given to someone during the vigil. (Note: there are cards for the living, as well, and these make nice gifts for special occasions for both Catholics and non-Catholics.)

The Roman Catholic church recognizes cremation with a memorial service that can be held at the church, mortuary or mausoleum. There would be no vigil or public rites of committal. A Mass card would be appropriate.

22.3 Orthodox Christianity

Orthodox Christianity consists of ancient traditions such as Greek, Russian, Armenian and Syrian. Cremation is not allowed for Orthodox Christianity and no funerals are performed for those who are to be cremated. The funeral service is quite elaborate and chanted by the priest and cantor (layperson assisting the priest in the service).

The casket is brought into the church, the body with feet first, and remains feet towards the alter during the service. It is a common practice to have an icon (religious portrait) of the resurrection of Christ (which Orthodox Christianity venerates as a reminder of death being conquered by Christ's resurrection) on a stand near the casket. The casket will be closed. At the end of the service the casket may be opened and mourners may file past.

A homily (sermon) is offered after the service, not so much to eulogize the deceased, but to offer hope and encouragement to the living. The interment will be after the service. It is common to have a short prayer service at the gravesite with everyone invited to attend. Often the family of the deceased will extend an invitation to the mourners to gather at a family or friend's home or parish hall for a memorial meal.

Calling or visiting the family of the deceased as well as offering flowers, memorial gifts and sympathy cards are acceptable. Subdued clothing for the funeral service, which is held in the church, is recommended.

22.4 Hindu

In India, there are a myriad of Hindu sects that are based on regional affiliations to deities and practices. Hindus have brought that aspect of the faith with them to the United States. Some Americans, not born in India, have embraced Hinduism as well.

Philosophically, regarding death, Hinduism is somewhat similar to Buddhism in that the frame of mind in which one puts oneself just prior to and at the moment of death will determine the state of being into which one enters "after-death." Hindu beliefs include reincarnation; all living things (not just humans) will regenerate after death into another living form. There are yogic teachings that instruct the dying person to close all the "doors of the senses," fix the consciousness at the heart-center and stabilize the breath in the head to facilitate the transition.

When a person of Hindu faith is dying, whether in a hospital or at home, visitors are welcome. In the United States funerals are common and it is usually the responsibility of the mortician to prepare the body for the funeral. A special washing of the body by the family may be done at the time of death. If there is no family, friends could be invited. A priest will lead prayers and chants with candles and incense.

The body is transported to a crematorium, sometimes by the family, as a Hindu does not usually consider burial. If there is to be a visitation at the crematorium (usually not done if there is a funeral at a mortuary), the body will be presented in a coffin, attended by the family. The visitation will last two to three hours. A visitor is not expected to stay but to pay respects to the deceased and the family.

Flowers may be brought and placed on the body, on the coffin or near it. Once you have paid your respects you may console the family. A couple of things one could say would be:

"We are grieving also."
"God will give peace to the soul."

Because of reincarnation beliefs (the deceased will return to earth as another being) it would be inappropriate to say the deceased, "is now in heaven" (and imply the deceased will stay there).

The visit should not last any longer than half an hour and the visitor is expected to leave. There will not be any kind of "formal" service at the visitation. Once everyone is gone the body will be cremated. It is not unusual for the family to light the fire.

Ten to twelve days after the cremation there will be a special Hindu rite near water, fresh or sea water, which would be similar to a memorial service. Non-Hindus are also invited to that service.

22.5 Islam

The followers of Islam are called "Muslims," which means "the submitter," and comes from the historical Abraham of ancient times who was willing to sacrifice his son twice for submission to his God.

Today there are Muslims in every continent and race with a variety of death ritual customs such as accepting condolences, flowers, incense, food and sermons. However, there is one custom that is for all Muslims: the obligation of the living to take care of the dead. The historical precedent for this is from the story of Cain and Abel, the sons of Adam and Eve, considered by several religions to be the first humans on earth. Cain slew Abel. God sent a sign that Cain was to bury Abel, hence the first burial.

The obligation of the living may be an individual or a whole community. There are three steps within this obligation. The first is the ritual absolution done through the washing of the body called *ghusl*.

During the last moments of life, when possible, the Koran (western spelling for *Quran*) is read to the dying person. Upon death the body is turned towards Mecca (in present day Saudi Arabia and considered sacred to Islam) with the feet closest to Mecca. The mouth and eyes are closed and the face covered, legs and arms straightened, the death is announced to friends and family. Plans are made to bathe the body, which is usually done at the mortuary. Islamic specifications decree that a man will wash a male and a woman will wash a female.

The second step is the shrouding of the body. This is done after the ritual bathing and two pieces of cloth are used — one piece for the lower half, the other for the upper, leaving the face exposed. Often the cloth used is white cotton. Islamic tradition urges the family of the deceased to call upon people who are trained in the bathing and shrouding of the deceased as a sign of respect.

The third obligation is the *janazah*, the funeral prayer, usually performed at the gravesite before burial. There are no clergy in Islam, but a religious advisor (cleric) may lead the prayer in which the mourners join.

Most Moslem funerals are held at the cemetery near the burial site, and the body is buried as quickly as possible after death. Male family members carry the casket. During the funeral, mourners may be very expressive with crying and wailing. Fainting may happen. The expressiveness found in Muslim funerals is part of the coping and attaining peace rituals, although some mosques frown upon the practice.

Moslem tradition does not include caskets but United States law does for burial. It is an un-Islamic custom to display the deceased in an open coffin or to bury one in an ornate casket. However, open casket funerals are not uncommon in the United States. Islam encourages the mourners to place a few handfuls of earth over the casket at the gravesite whenever possible.

The wearing of black clothing is not found in Islamic teachings but modest attire is recommended. Non-Muslims do not have to wear a head covering but it does add a sign of respect. After the burial friends and family may go to the deceased's home and usually a meal is provided.

Muslims believe that prayers offered for the deceased at the time of death and for days afterward will make it easier for the deceased in the afterworld. The mourning period is three days.

22.6 Jewish

In the Jewish tradition from the moment of death until burial, the deceased should not be left alone. Burial within 24 hours of death is preferred, and there is no viewing. Burial will be delayed to accommodate out-of-town relatives. The body is ritually washed and shrouded. A plain wooden box-type casket with no metal parts or decoration is preferred.

An ancient tradition, *Keriah*, the tearing of the garments of the mourners, is a cut or tear of just a few inches. The mourners are immediate family members. Tradition requires cutting through all garments over the heart. Some Reform families opt to cut a scarf or small ribbons. Each member of the immediate family then says a blessing.

Donations made in the deceased's name are preferred to floral tributes. Prior to the conclusion of the service, family, good friends, or the rabbi will eulogize the deceased.

At the funeral's conclusion, most of the people attending the funeral service (at a synagogue or mortuary) will join the procession to the grave. A Jewish tradition may have a processional from the hearse to the grave with all following the casket and there can be three or seven ritual pauses on the way. It is considered an offense to the deceased to turn away before the casket is lowered. The casket is lowered into the grave, and earth is symbolically thrown onto the casket. Orthodox and Conservative Jews may actually fill the grave entirely as part of the ceremony.

Proper cemetery etiquette means no eating or drinking, dressing respectfully, not stepping over or sitting upon gravestones that directly cover a grave. Flowers that have bloomed at the grave may not be picked for a keepsake.

The family recites a special mourner's *Kaddish*, a memorial prayer. Upon conclusion of this prayer, the friends will form two parallel lines for the family to walk through, back to their vehicles. The participants comfort the mourners with an eight-word chant as they pass between them. They do not look back, and will stop to rinse their hands at the roadside, thus cleansing themselves (a symbol of the ancient custom of purification) of the duties associated with caring for the deceased. The emphasis now shifts from the deceased to the concerns and comfort of the mourners.

Traditionally the family would sit *Shiva*, the initial intensive mourning period, for seven days following the burial. Reform Jews will sit three days. Other family members and friends may be invited to attend prayer services at the home mornings and evenings, during these seven days. People are encouraged to stop and visit with the family at this time.

Mourners are not supposed to return to the cemetery less than every 30 days so as not to grieve to excess. A monument is placed on the grave as soon as possible, so as not to have the grave unmarked, as that is doing a dishonor to the deceased. The monument placing is considered part of the funeral service, even though it occurs several weeks later. The major thrust at the "setting of a monument" is to eulogize the deceased. On the first anniversary of the death there is a ceremony as well.

22.7 Mormon

The Church of Jesus Christ Latter-Day Saints, as they are more formally known, has a well-defined approach to death and the afterlife. Their funeral services are usually rather calm affairs with family and friends of the deceased confident they will see the departed again in an afterlife.

Cremation is not encouraged. The deceased's body is dressed in a special garment. Viewing of the body is usually for one hour before the funeral service. The service often is longer than in other religions, with both eulogies and musical interludes. Family members and close friends will speak and provide music.

Mormon churches where the funeral services take place are not to be confused with the Mormon temples. The church is open to all, Mormons and non-Mormons alike. The temple is not.

If called upon to speak, please note the church specifically requests that it not be implied that the deceased will have a wonderful afterlife regardless of his or her conduct on the earth.

At the graveside a family member will also say a dedicatory prayer.

22.7 Protestant

There is a wide range of beliefs and sects from non-denominational to evangelical. That means there can be a wide range of traditions with everything from cremation to burial, elaborate funeral to no funeral at all.

While each has its own traditions, some general suggestions may be offered. Telephoning the bereaved with condolences before the funeral is usually acceptable as is visiting, sending flowers or a personal note. The visitor should keep the visit short rather than burdening the bereaved by staying too long. If you are not sure whether to bring food, ask the bereaved.

Appropriate attire for men is usually a jacket and tie. For women head covering is not required and common sense dictates that one dress respectfully as befitting the situation. Somber colors are recommended.

As to gifts, flowers and/or charitable donations are traditional, while monetary gifts to the bereaved are not.

Funeral services and interment are usually open to guests. The service may or may not include an open casket and it is an individual's choice whether to view the body. Cremation is becoming more popular with either a funeral before cremation or a memorial service after cremation.

22.9 Quaker

Based on testimonies of simplicity and equality, mourners gather for memorial services typified by silent worship interspersed with thoughtful prayers, reminiscences or expressions as "led by the Spirit." Cremation has become preferred in most communities. Non-Quakers are welcome to the service and may participate.

These are but a few of the cultures and religions practiced in the United States. Quite often people are afraid to say or do anything when the situation involves different cultures and religions. Fear of the unknown or of making a mistake can stop people from reaching out to one another. In today's multicultural times these fears are outdated as is being judgmental of another person's religion or culture.

Heartfelt communication is never in poor taste, and can ease grief and loss.

PART V
SPECIAL CIRCUMSTANCES

Casualty

He was a soldier in the army,
But he doesn't walk like one.
He walks like his soldiering
Days are done.

Son!...Son!

— Langston Hughes, writer
The Collected Poems of Langston Hughes

Military

"He gave me a smile. That was it."

— Bert Dowdy,
World War II Navy veteran

23.1 General Information for All Branches

There are five branches of the armed services: Army, Navy, Marine Corps, Air Force and Coast Guard. Burial and cremation are part of military funerals as well as burial at sea which the Navy offers.

23.1.1 Burial of Active Duty Personnel

In the case of death of an active-duty member the benefits are similar for all five branches. The military will notify the next-of-kin (NOK). Each branch has a department that handles next-of-kin notification, benefit information, and helping the next-of-kin through the funeral procedures. At the time of notification the next-of-kin will have to decide whether they wish to use the funeral home the branch has contracted with or use a funeral home of their choice. If burial is involved, the next-of-kin must also decide whether the deceased will be buried in a national or private cemetery.

23.1.2 Interment Flag

These flags have been authorized for use in military funerals by the Department of Veterans Affairs and are called the Veterans Affairs burial flag. These flags are supplied at no cost and are authorized for the funerals of active duty personnel, retirees and veterans. If the flag is to be used for a current funeral of an active duty deceased person the funeral home contracted for the funeral has the flag application form, can help you fill it out, and pick up the flag. This is not a free service by the funeral home.

To obtain one yourself, check with your local post office or Dept. of Veterans Affairs office, which is located at a federal building. Not all post offices carry these flags, so call first. The Veteran Affairs office phone number will be located in your phone book, white pages, in the front under the heading "Federal Government." If you are not successful locally, call the nearest authorized port listed. You will need to fill out the flag application form that you may obtain at the funeral home, V.A. or some post offices. You will need to show proof of military service of the deceased such as discharge or retirement documents and a death certificate.

If the request is on behalf of a Navy person and you are not successful locally, call the nearest authorized port listed in the "Sea Burial" section.

23.1.3 Active Duty Benefits
(these figures may fluctuate)

Civilian mortuary & private cemetery	$3,000
Government cemetery	$2,000
Coast Guard	$3,100

Full Honors, if possible to include 16 to 19 people (pallbearers)

23.1.4 Veteran's Burial Honors

One or two people present flag military style during funeral. It isn't guaranteed because of lack of personnel but one could request a rifle squad and bugler from the service the deceased served. for Some branches do once-a-month honors, which would be like a memorial service. If using a mortuary one would need to fill out the necessary documents and inform Veteran's Affairs. If doing this yourself contact the branch of service in which the deceased served.

Army suggestion during Army style funeral: "For the two volleys civilians put hand on heart, military will salute, keep on heart for taps."

23.2 Burial at Sea

The Navy offers the "Burial at Sea" program. All members of the uniformed services, including retired personnel and those honorably discharged, are eligible for burial at sea, along with their dependents.

23.2.1 Burial at Sea for Active-Duty Personnel

NAVY: If the active-duty deceased dies aboard a ship, even if the next-of-kin wishes a burial at sea, the remains will be brought to the nearest port and an autopsy performed before the burial at sea. If desired by the next-of-kin, the Navy will see to it that the deceased joins his/her ship for the burial at sea.

OTHER: the Navy runs Non-Navy branches burial-at-sea. The next-of-kin (NOK) would coordinate this with that branch's department responsible for body disposition.

23.2.2 Burial at Sea for Retired or Honorably Discharged Personnel

The majority of burials at sea are cremated remains and the family incurs little cost. The burial at sea of intact casketed remains, is not widely practiced because the remains must be prepared, shipped to a funeral home at the port, and stored, all of which the family must pay for.

Remains are sent to a burial-at-sea coordinator at an authorized Navy port with all associated documents. The coordinator requests permission from higher authority to identify a ship to carry out the burial. Since the burials are conducted during the ship's routine operations, it is not possible for the family to attend. One exception may be Pearl Harbor, Hawaii.

Once the vessel has been identified, the remains are delivered to a shipboard liaison. At some point during the ship's underway period, the skipper (commanding officer) calls the ship to full stop and orders the assembly of the burial detail. Members of the ship's crew may assist in the ceremony, such as the commanding officer/executive officer and chaplain. There is also a rifle squad and a bugler. The ceremony is basically the same as one at a cemetery.

After the services, the commanding officer sends a letter to the next of kin describing the details of the service along with nautical charts depicting the exact location of the burial, three cartridges from the rifle squad, and pictures, or if available, a video tape of the ceremony. If the interment flag was provided to the ship for the services, it will be returned to the family; if not, one will be used but will not be given to the family.

Navy style: "U.S. Citizens who are determined eligible by notable service or outstanding contributions to the United States". [Navy Military Funerals] This is for a full honors Navy style funeral as mandated by the Navy manual on Navy funerals.

23.2.3 Cost

For cremated remains the next of kin will be responsible for the cost of mailing the container to an authorized port. It is recommended that the packaged cremains be sent via certified mail, return receipt requested. For intact remains there is the cost of body preparation, transport container, storage and casket preparation at the authorized port, plus the services of a professional. The cost can be thousands of dollars.

23.2.4 Container

For cremains an urn or plastic or metal box must be used to prevent spillage in shipping to the port. For intact remains a transport container must be used and the casket used on the ship needs to be banded, holed, and weighted according to specific naval instructions.

23.2.5 Ports
There are five authorized ports; two Atlantic ports and three Pacific ports as listed. See the Appendix listed under "Ports For Military Burial At Sea".

23.2.6 Documents
For both intact and cremated remains the following forms are needed:
• Burial at Sea Request/Authorization form
• Photocopy of death certificate
• Burial transit permit or cremation certificate
• Copy of the DD Form 214, discharge certificate or retirement orders

The Navy will do its best in granting the next-of-kin their wishes for the final disposition. The cremains of a former naval aviator were waiting in Hawaii. The spouse wanted him buried at sea off a naval aircraft carrier in the Hawaii area. Aircraft carriers are not attached in Hawaii, they just come through now and then. The next time a carrier came through on its way to a naval exercise, the naval coordinator for the burial at sea program in Hawaii made sure the cremains were aboard. The spouse was not impatient. She understood some wishes could take a little longer than usual.

Pearl Harbor, Hawai'i: Only service people on the island of O'ahu, Hawai'i, at the time of the December 7, 1941 Pearl Harbor bombing, and their spouses, are allowed a Navy style internment of cremated remains in Pearl Harbor. Any service is eligible.

Fire Service

"You learn to trust...rely on each other...become
family...can become more than real family as [the] real
family not understand...develop a close link...death like
losing a family member, sometimes even closer."

— Terence Francis,
Fire Marshall, City of Burlington, VT

There are approximately 350,000 full time career fire service people in the U.S., and adding volunteers the ranks swell to 2.2 million overall. The fire service defines "in the line of duty" as someone who dies while fire fighting, while "active duty" can be death by other than fire fighting. The size of a city and the resources available dictate what is done when there is a death of a fire fighter. Some places are so small that whether the person was on duty or retired, the final arrangements are the same.

The following is general information for the public.

24.1 Killed in the line of duty

- The body is removed by members of the deceased's company to the coroner.
- The fire chief and fellow fire service friends do in-person notification to the nearest of kin. (NOK)
- A department liaison will stay with the family, if they wish.
- Family wishes are followed. If the family doesn't want a funeral, a memorial service will be requested by the fire department.
- Benefits, reimbursement and relief funds are arranged.

24.2 Funeral

- The amount of equipment is determined by how much is available at the time of the funeral.
- The deceased, if burial is to be done, will be borne in the coffin on the fire truck most closely associated with the deceased.
- The cortège, made up of fire trucks and other vehicles, officials and family, will wend its way from the funeral service to the burial site, often passing the firehouse associated with the deceased. It is not unknown for the cortège to be several miles long.
- All firefighter companies that are able to attend the funeral or funeral cortège will do so.
- The funeral/memorial services may be open to the public that is up to the family. The cortége is considered public and often people will line up on the street for the cortége. If one is out and a cortége passes, one may salute, put one's hand on the heart, or stand quietly until the cortége has passed. If in your car it is considered quite rude to honk, either as a commemoration or because you are impatient. For a large cortége public announcements through newspaper/radio will let the public know the route of the cortége.

History of Los Angeles Fire Bell — The bell, donated to the historical collection of the Relief Association by Retired Fireman Frank Bontempo, was once the dinner bell at old Fire Station 4, located at 227 E. Aliso Street. The iron hook on the top of the bell was used to suspend it from a water pipe in the unfinished basement kitchen. Legend has it that the unusual color of the bell was due to its being burned in a fire that destroyed the Fire Dept Storeroom located behind the fire station. Salvaged from the debris, the bell called members at mealtime until 1948 when the station closed.

Law Enforcement

"People forget how many we lost, too"

— Distraught spokesperson for
the New York Port Authority
speaking of 9/11 loss
of NYPA personnel

Law enforcement includes police, FBI, Justice, Port Authorities, Sheriffs, Immigration and some armed services in the community. Much of the procedure, killed in the line of duty and the funeral is similar with the fire service. The funeral cortége is often viewed by the public, even televised. The funeral service, for both the fire service and law enforcement is usually by invitation only.

The Bagpipe Tradition

One of the oldest and most sacred of traditions is that of the lone piper playing "Amazing Grace" at the gravesite of the fallen officer. The lone piper has become synonymous with the police and firefighter funeral.

The bagpipes, as an invention, can be traced back to biblical times, with credit for European distribution given to the Roman Legions, who provided the 'pipes to the warrior tribes of Ireland, Scotland, and Britannia. Refined in Ireland, but really liked by the Scots, the bagpipes became an instrument of war and of final peace.

With a few modifications this strange musical instrument landed in America via the many Irish and Scottish immigrants who left the old country to find a better life in America, The big cities were hiring though, and dangerous jobs as police officers and firemen were plentiful, especially in places like Boston, New York, and Chicago. Those that didn't like the big like big city life headed west and south, for places like Gettysburg, Little Bighorn, and Texas;

where it was John McGregor, a Scotsman, who played the pipes during the siege of the Alamo.

The heavily Irish NYPD officers, formed the first Police Emerald Society, an Irish-American fraternal organization in 1953. Subsequently, the Emerald Society's Pipe and Drum bands started there and has spread all over the U.S. Today, the Emerald Society Memorial Pipeband March is an integral part of National Police Memorial Week ceremonies in Washington, DC every year, featuring hundreds of law enforcement pipers and drummers from all over the nation. Only the massed bands of the British Army rivals this truly spectacular event. It is from the ranks of these officers that the solo piper is usually drawn to play the police funerals.

This bagpipe history is from Detective Brian Leighton, Texas Emerald Society, by way of Jim Sanfilippo, First Vice President of Law Enforcement Emerald Societies.

On the famous Native American Indian Chief
Geronimo's death certificate, which was called a "death
return" in 1909, under the space of "Occupation"
the person who filled out the document has written
"None," and his name is listed as "Chief Geronimo."

— February 18, 1909

Famous People

"Clark Gable, mega movie star of the '40s and '50s, died of a heart attack in 1960. He had served in the Army Air Corp during World War II as a pilot; he was attended with full military honors. He is buried at Forest Lawn Memorial Park, Los Angeles, beside his third wife, Carole Lombard."

— Solitude in Stone newsletter

When famous people die newspeople are interested as well as the public. Persons responsible for the famous deceased person have the additional responsibility of balancing the needs of the survivors of the deceased and the wants of the public and news media.

For example, when Marilyn Monroe died in 1962, it was her ex-husband, famous ballplayer, Joe DiMaggio who stepped in to handle the arrangements. In addition to arranging the funeral he banned all "Hollywood friends" and the Kennedy family from the funeral. While there were only 31 mourners at the actual funeral, thousands of fans were outside the Westwood Memorial Park Chapel and Mr. DiMaggio would have had to help arrange for police protection as well as traffic control.

Another famous, or one could say "infamous" death was John Gotti, known as the "Dapper Don" which alluded to his sartorial splendor and his vocation, that of belonging to the Mafia. Arrested and in jail for his lifetime, he contracted cancer and died in prison in 2002.

No longer alive and therefore not a threat to society, Mr. Gotti was allowed to leave prison. His family was allowed to proceed with funeral arrangements. The flower arrangements sent to the family are legendary in their variety and creativity.

State Funerals

"There are few events in our national life that unite
Americans and so touch the hearts of all of us as the
passing of a President of the United States"

— Earl Warren,
Chief Justice of the United States,
eulogy of John F. Kennedy,
assassinated U.S. president

State funerals are funerals for heads of state such as presidents, royalty and dignitaries who are afforded the trappings of a state funeral. The actual funeral is almost always closed to the public, but almost everything else is very public. All of the arrangements are a combination of protocol, tradition and the wishes of the survivors.

An interesting example was the music that was used for President Kennedy's funeral. A combination of protocol ("Hail to the Chief"), tradition ("Ruffles and Flourishes"), and personal wishes ("O God of Loveliness") and planned to the minute. This was done for all the services at the Capitol, the White House, the Cathedral and Arlington National Cemetery. It was 1962 and the nation was able to watch on television.

In 1999, Missouri Governor Mel Carnahan, running for a Senate seat, was killed when the small airplane he was in crashed. His wife and family had the stress of planning a funeral while coping with the sudden death of loved ones. Additionally there had to be thought of how to acknowledge the public. The always poignant "Missing Man" flying formation by the Missouri Air National Guard was impressive and seen by thousands at the site and many more on television.

Mrs. Carnahan went on to become Missouri's Senator.

APPENDIX

An Atlanta entrepreneur has begun selling Eternal Reefs, which he makes by mixing cremated remains and concrete to form a 3,000 pound artificial reef, which can be dropped into the ocean to create a new ecosystem. Inventor Don Brawley says the underwater urns cost $850 to $3,200, depending on whether the deceased wants to swim with the fishes solo or join a communal graveyard.

— Found on the Internet

GLOSSARY

Administrator
A person named by the court to execute a deceased person's estate when the deceased does not leave a will.

Anticipatory grief
Process of mourning begun before the death of a person actually occurs.

Attending Physician
A doctor that you have established a relationship with, who knows your medical history and has medical records of your medical history. Also called a "family doctor." Also is the primary doctor for the deceased or the doctor who signs the death certificate.

Authorized Agent
The person or persons entitled to the control of the disposition of a deceased person.

Autopsy/Postmortem
Examination of dead body to determine the cause of death or origins of disease.

Benefactor
The person who originally sets up a living trust.

Bereavement
The state of feeling loss.

Bereavement Fare
Discounted passenger fare offered by airlines and trains for individuals accompanying a deceased's body in transit. Airlines may also offer this fare for individuals needing emergency travel due to critical illness or death.

Biopsy
The removal and examination of tissues, cells, or fluids from a living body as an aid to medical diagnosis and/or treatment.

Brain Dead

The lower part of the brain that controls breathing and other bodily processes is not functioning.

Cardiac Arrest

Heart stoppage commonly called a "heart attack."

Casket

A receptacle or encasement in which the body is placed for a funeral ceremony and final disposition above or below ground. The word "coffin" is a somewhat outdated terminology of a case, chest or box in which a dead person is placed for burial.

Cemetery

A place intended and dedicated for the disposition of dead human (as well as pet) remains. Also called a "graveyard."

Columbarium

A building constructed with niches to house cremated remains.

Committal

A final ceremony usually held at the grave or place of final disposition. Commonly called a "graveside" ceremony.

Consignee

The name of the funeral provider who will be providing necessary preparation and documentation for the transport of human remains from another country. Also called "receiver of human remains."

Contingency-Day Planning

At least a once-a-year plan and review of all financial and legal matters

Coroner/Medical Examiner

A public official whose legal responsibility is to investigate any death suspected to have resulted from other than natural causes.

Corpse

A dead human body.

Cremation

The process of reducing the human body to bone fragments and particles through the use of intense heat and flame.

Cremation Authorization Form

A legal form giving permission to cremate human remains signed by the next of kin or person(s) entitled by law to control disposition.

Cremation Chamber

An enclosed space within which the cremation of human remains takes place.

Cremation Container

A combustible, closed container resistant to the leakage of bodily fluids into which the decedent is placed before insertion in a cremation chamber.

Cremated Remains (Cremains)

Human remains after the completion of the cremation process.

Crematory

A building or structure that houses an incinerator for reducing human remains.

Crepe

Fabric worn or draped on a doorway as a sign of mourning.

Cryogenics

The freezing of anything.

Cryonics

The science of low-temperature preservation of the human body and/or body parts for future use.

Cryonic suspension

The act of keeping a human body or body part preserved for eventual revival.

Crypt

A chamber (underground or above ground) used as a burial place.

Death Benefit

An entitlement payable to the authorized beneficiary.

Death Certificate

Official record of a death filed with the state government.

Death Notice

A paid advertisement announcing a death, usually in a newspaper.

Death Wish

The conscious or unconscious desire for death of oneself or someone else.

Deceased/Decedent (noun)
Dead person.

Decomposition
The natural process of bodily decay.

Defibrillation
Restoring rhythm to a heart by electric shock via a machine with paddles that are placed on the chest.

Disinterment
The act of removing human (or pet) remains from a grave.

Disposition
The interment, entombment, shipment, scattering, or release of human remains.

Disposition Permit
A legal document issued by the county health department before final disposition of the body can be made including burial, cremation, entombment and shipment.

Durable Power of Attorney For Health Care/Proxy
A competent person formally designates someone to make medical/health decisions on their behalf should the competent person lose the capacity to make their own decisions.

Electrocardiogram (EKG)
The recording of changes of electrical potential taking place during the heartbeat used in diagnosing abnormalities.

Electroencephalogram (EEG)
The recording of brain waves.

Embalming
The process of treating the dead human body to reduce the presence and growth of microorganisms, to retard organic decomposition, and to restore an acceptable physical appearance from the ravages of trauma and illness.

Entombment
The placement of human remains in a crypt in a mausoleum.

Epitaph
A funeral oration. An inscription on or at a tomb in memory of the one buried there. A brief statement worded as if to be inscribed on a monuments.

Estate

The assets and liabilities of a person at his/her death.

Eulogy

Speech of recognition or remembrance for the deceased.

Euthanasia

The act or method of causing death painlessly, so as to end suffering.

Execu(tor/trix)

A legal term, the person appointed by the owner of a Will to carry out the terms of the Will after the owner of the Will is deceased. Commonly called a "personal representative."

Funeral Director/Funeral Practitioner/Undertaker/Mortician

Licensed professional who manages all aspects of deceased body disposition. "Undertaker" and "Mortician" are older traditional titles while "Funeral Director" and "Funeral Practitioner" are more modern.

Funeral Home/Funeral Parlor/Mortuary

Which name is used depends somewhat on geographic location in the United States.

Funeral Mass

A Catholic ritual of church service.

Funeral Service/Ceremony

Observances and rites held for the dead before burial or cremation.

General Price List

A printed list that contains the cost of individual funeral items and various services offered by a funeral provider.

Grave

A space in the ground in which to bury a dead body or a burial mound or monument. Also known as a "plot."

Grief

Spontaneous expression of thoughts, feelings, and behavior in response to a loss.

Hearse

A specialized vehicle for conveying the dead. Also known as a "coach."

Heroic Measures

Medical machinery and practices used to prolong life.

Hospice

A place for the terminally ill to reside and be tended until their death which usually may not exceed six months.

Identifying

The act of positive recognition of a deceased person.

Immortality

Exemption from death.

Interment

Disposition of human remains by entombment or burial in a cemetery, or with cremated remains, by inurnment, placement, burial in a cemetery or burial at sea.

International Repatriation

The transport of human remains from one country to another.

Intestate

A person dying without having left a Will. Each state makes very specific provisions for the settling of an estate when someone dies intestate.

Intubation

A medical procedure in which a tube is placed in the mouth to assist or facilitate breathing.

Inurnment

Placing cremated remains in a cremated remains container (urn) suitable for placement, burial, shipment, or holding of said cremated remains.

Kaddish

A Jewish prayer recited after the death of a friend or relative.

Last Rites

Religious or non-religious rituals for the purpose of easing the transition from life to death.

Living Trust

A legal document as a way to avoid probate time and expenses. A legal concept created in medieval England for the purpose of escaping death taxes.

Living Will (see "Medical Directive")

Mausoleum

A building that contains crypts to house human remains.

Medical Directive

A document in which competent people try to contemplate what medical interventions they would want or not want should they lose mental/physical capacity in the future. May also include the naming of "Durable Power of Attorney for Health Care" person and their responsibilities; ombudsman witness (if entering a facility) and other such documents as a "Do Not Resuscitate" forms. It is generally regarded as a legal document unlike the older version which was called "Living Will."

Memorialization

An event, thing, or place meant to help people remember the deceased, such as a gathering, monument, marker, grave or niche.

Memorial Ceremony

A gathering of people at a specific location, generally without the decedent's body present.

Minimum Care

A basic level of professional care rendered to the body of a deceased person prior to disposition, including but not limited to refrigeration and storage.

Monument

Something generally of a permanent nature erected in remembrance of the dead. Also called a "headstone" or "tombstone."

Mourning

Expression of grief including ritual, ceremony, and other social, religious, and ethnic activity due to loss.

Niche

A space in a columbarium used for the placement of cremated remains in an urn.

Nitrogen Cycle

A continuous series of natural processes by which nitrogen passes through successive stations in air, soil, and organisms; a cycle of growth, death, decay, and reuse by new organisms.

Obituary (also called "necrologue" or "necrology")

A notice in a publication, video or Internet of a person's death, usually with a short biographical account. A professional obituary writer is called a "necrologue" or "necrographer."

Organ Transplant

To transfer an organ or tissue from one individual to another.

Outer Burial Container

A grave liner generally made of concrete or other rigid material to encapsulate the casket and to prevent the earth from caving in or washing away. Often called a "vault."

Pall

A cloth draped over a casket as a part of a religious ceremony.

Pallbearer

A person who helps carry a casket at a funeral.

Palliative Care

Medical care for the terminally ill that focuses on relieving the pain and making the patient comfortable.

Pathological Incinerator

The designated technical term used by the Environmental Protection Agency to describe a cremation chamber.

Persistent Vegetative State

The upper part of the brain, the cortex, is inactive which produces unconsciousness.

Petition

Upon intestate (no will), asking the court for something. This procedure costs money and there are paperwork hassles.

Planning Ahead

Also called "pre-need" or "advance planning" by the funeral profession, is the act of completing and organizing in writing one's funeral and final disposition before one's death.

Postdeath Contact

Parapsychological (not scientifically based) experiences related to inter-action between the living and the dead in some sensory mode (hearing, seeing, feeling) usually shortly after death occurs.

Probate

After death the assets and liabilities (what you have and what you owe) of the deceased are immediately frozen until a will is proven to be authentic or intestacy (no will) matters are settled in the Superior Court of the county in which the deceased lived at the time of their death.

Procession

A group of people, vehicles or objects moving along in an orderly, possibly formal manner.

Processing

The removal of foreign objects and the reduction of cremated remains by mechanical means to reduce them to a manageable consistency for inurnment.

Property

In a legal sense, something that is capable of being owned.

Putrefaction

The decomposition of any organic matter such as a human body.

Registrar

Official state government office where death certificates and other legal documents are filed.

Reincarnation

A rebirth in a new body or form of life (religious/philosophical inter-pretation).

Remains

The body of a deceased person including cremated fragments and particles.

Restoration

During the embalming process of a human being the removal of dev-astation caused by long-term diseases, illnesses, or trauma, and removal of disfigurement created by the long-term usage of therapeutic drugs, and removal of the visible postmortem changes that may have begun to appear.

Resuscitation

The revival from apparent death or unconsciousness.

Ritualization

A gathering of people to observe or practice a prescribed ceremonial procedure, generally religious/spiritual in custom.

Scattering

The authorized dispersal of cremated remains at sea, or in a defined area within cemetery grounds.

Scattering Gardens

A defined area within cemetery grounds for cremated remains.

Shiva

Jewish seven or three-day period of formal mourning following the funeral of a close relative or loved one.

Shraddha

A Hindu ceremony held 10 to 30 days after death intended to liberate the soul of the deceased

Shroud

Cloth or ritual garments used to wrap a body for burial.

Soul

Non material spiritual essence of an individual life (religious/philosophical interpretation).

Springing Durable Power of Attorney

Takes legal effect upon the happening of an event, usually the incapacity of the person creating the power. Gives the agent power to provide financial and legal decisions for the person who has become incapacitated.

Statutory

State-specific laws pertaining to an individual state.

Successor Trustee

Individual(s) and/or organization named by a benefactor in a living trust.

Suspended Animation

The cessation of atomic movement (pertaining to cryonic suspension of a human body).

Thanatology

The study of death and dying

Urn

A specially designed receptacle used to hold cremated remains.

Urn Garden

A defined area within a cemetery for the placement of an urn into the ground or other structure within the garden, such as a wall niche.

Urn Vault

An outside support receptacle into which an urn is placed prior to earth burial.

Vault

Made out of cement/metal, encapsulates the casket to protect it from earth movement and water.

Viewing/Visitation/Calling Hours

The act of gathering at a funeral home, private home or church to pay one's respects and to say good-bye to a deceased person.

Wake

Staying with the body prior to the funeral, or the ritual of visitation proceeding the funeral.

A gathering at a survivor's home or funeral home with food and drink to "celebrate" the deceased's life.

Widow

A woman whose spouse has died.

Widower

A man whose spouse has died.

Will

A person's intentions as to their wishes for all of their assets and debts as they relate family members and others. The Will is in some form of print, video, CD or film, and is to be used after the person's death.

The American Dialect Society, which annually announces its prizes for words and terms introduced into the English language, has declared that for 1997 the prize for the most euphemistic word went to: "EXIT BAG: bag placed over one's head to commit suicide."

Federal Trade Commission Funeral Rule

This rule, established in 1984, enables consumers to obtain information about funeral arrangements and includes such things as:

Telephone Price Disclosures
When phoning a funeral provider about terms, conditions, or prices of funeral goods or services, the provider will:

- Tell you that price information is available over the telephone.
- Give you prices and any other information from the price lists to reasonably answer your questions.
- Give you any other information that is readily available.

General Price List
If you inquire in person about funeral arrangements, the funeral provider will give you a general price list, which you may keep.

Embalming Information
Requires funeral providers to give consumers information about embalming that may help consumers decide whether to purchase this service:

- May not falsely state that embalming is always required by law.
- May not charge a fee for unauthorized embalming unless it is required by state law.
- Will disclose in writing that you usually have the right to choose a disposition such as a direct cremation or immediate burial if you do not want embalming.

- Will disclose to you in writing that certain funeral arrangements such as a funeral with a viewing may make embalming a practical necessity and thus a required purchase.

Cash Advance Sales

- Requires funeral providers to disclose to you in writing if they charge a fee for buying cash advance items. Cash advance items are goods or services that are paid for by the funeral provider on your behalf. Some examples of cash advance items are flowers, obituary notices, pallbearers, and clergy honoraria (fee). Some funeral providers charge you their cost for these items. Others add a service fee to their cost.

- The Funeral Rule requires the funeral provider to inform you when a service fee is added to the price of cash advance items, or if the provider gets a refund, discount, or rebate from the supplier of any cash advance item.

Caskets For Cremation

Funeral providers who offer cremation without ceremony or viewing:

- Must not tell you that state or local law requires a casket for cremations.

- Must disclose in writing your right to buy an unfinished wood box (a type of casket) or an alternative container for cremation.

- Must make an unfinished wood box or alternative container available for cremation.

Required Purchases
You do not have to purchase unwanted goods or services as a condition of obtaining those you do want unless required by state law:

- You have the right to choose only the funeral goods and services you want, with some disclosed exceptions.

- The funeral provider must disclose this in writing on the general price list.

- The funeral provider must disclose on your itemized statement of goods and services selected the specific state law that requires you to purchase any particular item.

Statement Of Funeral Goods And Services Selected
The funeral provider will give you an itemized statement of the total cost of the funeral goods and services you select. This statement will also disclose any legal, cemetery, or crematory requirements that compels you to purchase any specific funeral goods or services.

Preservative And Protective Claims
Funeral providers are prohibited from telling you a particular funeral item or service can indefinitely preserve the body of the deceased in the grave:

- May not claim embalming or a particular type of casket will indefinitely preserve the deceased's body.

- Prohibits funeral providers from making claims that funeral goods, such as caskets or vaults, will keep out water, dirt, and other gravesite substances when that is not true.

State Vital Statistics Offices
With Cost Of Death Certificate

Each state has its own rules and regulations for obtaining a death certificate such as your relation to the deceased or why you want the certificate. Some want a notarized statement. Make sure you call and ask exactly what is needed in order to obtain a death certificate. By the way, this goes for birth certificates as well.

State	Phone Number	Cost of Death Certificate
Alabama	205-242-5033	$12, $4 each add'l.
Alaska	907-465-3391	$7, $2 each add'l.
Arizona	602-255-3260	$5
Arkansas	501-661-2336	$4, $1 each add'l.
California	916-445-2684	$8
Colorado	303-338-6111	$12
Connecticut	203-566-2334	$5
Delaware	302-739-4721	$5, $3 each add'l.
District of Columbia	202-727-9281	$12
Florida	904-354-3961	$5
	904-359-6900 FAX	
Georgia	404-656-4900	$10, $5 each add'l.*
	404-651-9427	*when ordered at same time
Hawaii	808-586-4533	$2
Idaho	208-334-5988	$8
Illinois	217-782-6553	$15, $2 each add'l.
Indiana	317-633-0274	$6, $1 each add'l.*
		*when ordered at same time
Iowa	515-281-4944	$6
Kansas	913-296-1404	$7, $5 each add'l.
Kentucky	502-564-4212	$6
Louisiana	504-568-5152	$5 Certified copy
		$2 burial transit permit
Maine	207-289-3184	$10, $4 each add'l.
Maryland	301-224-5988	$4

State	Phone Number	Cost of Death Certificate
Massachusetts	617-727-7388	$6 in person, $11 by mail
Michigan	517-335-8655	$13
Minnesota	612-623-5121	$8, $2 each add'l.
Mississippi	601-960-7981	$10, $2 each add'l.
Missouri	314-751-6381 314-751-6010 FAX	$10, $3 each add'l.
Montana	406-444-2614	$10
Nebraska	402-471-2871	$7
Nevada	702-885-4480	$8
New Hampshire	603-271-4654	$10, $6 each add'l.
New Jersey	609-292-4087	$4
New Mexico	505-827-0121	$5
New York City	212-619-4530	$5
New York State	518-474-8187	$15
North Carolina	919-733-3526	$10
North Dakota	701-224-2360	$5, $2 each add'l.
Ohio	614-466-2531	$7
Oklahoma	405-271-4040	$5
Oregon	503-731-4095 503-234-8417 FAX	$15, $12 each add'l.
Pennsylvania	412-852-5040 800-852-5040 (PA only) 412-656-3272 FAX	$3
Rhode Island	401-277-2811	$10, $5 each add'l.
South Carolina	803-734-4830	$8, $3 each add'l.
South Dakota	605-224-3355	$5
Tennessee	615-741-1763	$5
Texas	512-458-7111	$9, $3* *when ordered at same time
Utah	801-538-6380	$9, $5 each add'l.
Vermont	802-863-7275	$5
Virginia	804-786-6228	$5
Washington	206-753-5936	$11
West Virginia	304-558-2931	$5
Wisconsin	608-266-1371	$10, $2 each add'l.
Wyoming	307-777-7591	$6

Ports For Military Burial At Sea
Ports For Burial At Sea

Atlantic Ports

Norfolk, Virginia
Commanding Office
Attn: Code 0210C
Naval Medical Center

620 John Paul Jones Circle
Portsmouth, VA 23708-5100
Phone: 757-953-5573/5585

Jacksonville, Florida
Officer in Charge
Naval Hospital Branch Clinic
Naval Station

Mayport, FL 32228
Phone: 904-270-5301/6939/7296

Pacific Ports

San Diego, California
Commanding Officer
Naval Medical Center
San Diego, CA 92134-5000
ATTN: CODE 22-BAS
Phone: 619-532-8066
        1-800-290-7410
NOTE: requires $7 check or
money order made out to
County of San Diego.

Bremerton, Washington
Commanding Officer
Naval Hospital
Bremerton, WA 98312-5008
ATTN: CODE 015-DA
Phone: 306-475-4387/4303

Honolulu, Hawaii
Navy Liaison Unit
Tripler Army Medical Center
Tripler AMC, HI 96859-5000
Phone: 808-433-6611

Resources For The Reader

There are literally hundreds of books relating to death and dying. Computer related resources are popping up on a daily bases and pamphlets can be found at any death related business or organization. This book is not attempting to list every resource available. That in itself would make for a very big book, and a book that would be out of date soon as these resources change as time goes by. For up-to-date resources go online and visit the Death & Dying Information Center web site: www.the-ddic.com

This listing is to serve as a starting point for those who wish to pursue this topic in depth. For the reader who wants help but does not have the time for additional resource checking this listing provides general information that would be helpful.

This is a compilation of computer related items, books, pamphlets, and organizations that might be of interest to you. No promotion of any information provided is intended. However all organizations have been contacted that appear in this book and all printed/computer information has been checked for authenticity.

Computer Related
Computer Programs

Computer programs listed are those that relate to programs that can provide the reader with information, help create a document that can be used in preparing for a future death.

The first program is designed specifically for writing wills and health care directives. Both the latter two programs are general purpose legal programs. There are many software programs on the market, these are just three samples.

WillMaker6
Will-making software program for DOS, Windows or Macintosh, $69.95, Nolo Press in Berkeley, California (800-992-6656). Available at bookstores.

Kiplinger's Home Legal Advisor
Helps you create more than 65 legal documents. Does not need a CD-ROM drive, uses three discs. Windows95. $29.95, available from Block Financial Software. Orders: 800-813-7965.

Quicken Family Lawyer
Provides 76 different documents by category. $29.00, Parsons Technology. Orders: 800-679-0670

Internet
Web Sites

http://www.e-legal.com/
Electronic Legal Source offers many documents free and able to print out if one has a printer.

http://www.lawlinks,com/
Lawlinks, self-help offers resources for both consumers and attorneys

http://law.net/usalaw/index.htm
USA Law Publications offers a wide range of legal documents that one can fill out while one is on-line.

http://www.help4srs.com
Healthcare and Elder Law Programs Corporation, HELP, located in Southern California, through its web site offers discussion, legal documents, aids, articles, newsletter and resource links. Textured gray background distracting to reading text.

This is a non-profit information resource for Older Adults
and their helping friends and family members, providing
information, planning and problem-solving services focusing
on legal and healthcare-related issues that specially impact
Older Adults.

http://www.cmhc.com/selfhelp
The American Self-Help Clearinghouse has an online database
of international and national groups that include addresses and
phone numbers. There are over 1,000 listings.

http://www.funeral.com
(with additional URLs)
Funeral Service Center ™ (Bulletin Board), Funeral Service Center,™
Real Time (chat area), E-Mail Comments (keep in touch), Press
Releases, Suggestions, Professional E-Mail Correspondence
Exchange

http://www.cremation.org
Internet Cremation Society is an online advertising & marketing
medium for cremation and cremation related businesses with different death related links. Good site.

http://www.worldgardens.com/
A business, World Gardens, Inc. is a virtual cemetary. Free and fee
services. Graphics and sound.

http://www.amazon.com
A "virtual" retail bookstore with over two million book titles available for sale. There are dozens of titles related to death and dying,
many with descriptive sentences.

http://www.nolo.com
Publisher of books, pamphlets, tapes and software on a variety of
topics. Free catalog available.

http://www.growthhouse.org
Award-winning website provides an extensive international directory of end-of-life resources and offers a free monthly email
newsletter. (see "E-mail" below)

http://www.acponline.org/public/homecare
American College of Physicians Home Care Guide for Advanced
Cancer. Excellent site, easy to access and read. Covers area such as
understanding the problem, when to get professional help, what
you can do to help, possible obstacles, carrying out and adjusting
the plan. For those who don't have a computer, someone with a
computer can download the entire site in printed form. Just give
the person with the computer the above URL address.

http://travel.state.gov
(FAX 202-647-3000)
U.S. State Department offers Bureau of Consular Affairs
publications to help in the planning of a safer trip abroad.
Consular officers and agents provide assistance to Americans who
encounter emergencies while out of the country.

Concluding the most sensational medical investigation in
local history, the Riverside county coroner's office
announced Friday that Gloria R. died of kidney failure as a
result of cervical cancer — and the fumes that sickened
the emergency room staff tending her probably were
simply the smell of death.

— Radio, television & newspapers

Printed Material
Books

These are books that might be of help either as a practical "need-to-know" type of book or they could help a person's understanding of death, either their own or someone else's. Please note these are not the only books on the topic, just some suggestions. The "Reference" chapter following this chapter list all the references used in the writing of this book and may provide additional resources for the reader.

Death to Dust: What Happens to Dead Bodies by Kenneth Iserson, 1994, Galen Press Ltd., Hardcover $38.95. Available at bookstores, Web site Amazon.com.

> A several hundred page description of exactly what is embalming, what happens during an autopsy, funerals, cremation, cryogenics, etc. Some find it too detailed, other readers love it. Very informative and interesting.

Everybody Dies: A Guide to Final Arrangements by Jim Partridge, Partridge Publications, $14.95 + $2 for S&H; Order: 1-800-218-7033.

> Self-published softcover with some practical easy-to-read suggestions, helpful hints.

Final Curtain: Eternal Resting Places of Hundreds of Stars, Celebrities, Moguls, Misers & Misfits by Margaret Buck & Gary Hudson, 1996, Seven Locks Press, Softcover, $18.95. Order: 1-800-354-5348. Also at bookstores, Web site Amazon.com.

> For a break in planning your own funeral — a guide to the final resting place of hundreds of stars in southern California with sections on "death styles of the rich and famous", famous last lines, self-epitaphs, movie eulogies and humorous death-related quotations, etc. Fun.

Helping Children Cope with Death by Joan Singleton Prestine, 1994, Fearon (Simon and Schuster). Order: 1-800-242-7272, 1-800-775-1900

> Award winning author has two books. This is for parents, teachers, therapists or any adult to use with children to help them cope with their loss. Issues such as when to talk about the death, what to say, how children may react, and how may you react are sample topics. Easy-to-use format with more than fifty activities for children to help them with their feelings.
>
> Someone Special Died is a picturebook about a little girl who loses someone very special to her and how she comes to terms with her loss. It is designed to help children identify and deal with the various stages of mourning following the death of a loved one.

How to Be a Perfect Stranger: A Guide to Etiquette in Other People's Religious Ceremonies edited by Arthur J. Magida, 1996, Jewish Lights Publishing.

> An excellent, interesting, informative read. Twenty different religions are addressed and each religion has a section on "Funerals and Mourning". Available in bookstores.

How We Die by Sherwin Nuland, M.D., 1994, Alfred A. Knopf.

> A national best-seller, Dr. Nuland describes how a person dies from various diseases. A good read.

Nolo's Simple Will Book by Denis Clifford, Nolo Press, $17.95.

> Directions and forms for writing a simple will.

The Nuts and Bolts of Surviving the Loss or the Illness of a Loved One by Barbara T. Cochrane, BS, and Helen F. McGrane, PhD, 1990, $14.95 + $2.00 S&H

Regenesis Publishing, P.O. Box 11353, Burbank, CA 91510-1353
> A 133 page book with a 40 page format for maintaining a list of all the essential information needed by an individual. A little overwhelming and sometimes hard to understand but good to use as a format guide. Good letter formats. Geared for the middle-class who speak or understand English. There are some mistakes in the "Final Arrangements" chapter. Some redundancy and repetition.

Tibetan Book of Living and Dying by Sogyal Rimpoche, 1993, Harper: San Francisco.
> As described by the Dalai Lama in its foreword, "This book offer readers not just a theoretical account of death and dying, but also practical reasons for understanding, and for preparing themselves and others in a calm and fulfilling way."

When A Child Dies by Bonnie Hunt Conrad, 1995, Fithian Press, P.O. Box 15102, Santa Barbara, CA 93102. Order: 1-800-662-8351, $8.95
> Easy-to-read, short (56 pages) on what parents are going through after the death of a child, as well as what the people around them can do and say to the grieving parents.

Two Books For Unmarried Couples

A Legal Guide for Lesbian and Gay Couples by Hayden Curry, Denis Clifford & Robin Leonard, Nolo Press

Financial Self-Defense for Unmarried Couples by Larry M. Elkin, paperback, Doubleday.

Trust-Estate Planning

60 Minute Estate Planner by Sandy F. Kraemer, Prentice Hall, $18.95.

Make Your Own Living Trust by Denis Clifford, Nolo Press, $19.95.

Leaving Money Wisely by David Belin, Macmillan Publishing, $21.00.

> These books do not replace a lawyer when a lawyer is needed but can be used if estate is simple or to use as reference before meeting with a lawyer.

Funeral Professional tip: When trying to remove rings from a deceased person, thread a string under the ring leaving one end longer which is wrapped tightly around the finger. Begin unwrapping the shorter end of the string and the ring should slip off.

Pamphlets

There are dozens, if not hundreds, of pamphlets written about death, dying and grief. Many of the organizations listed in this chapter offer all kinds of pamphlets and they are not listed under "Pamphlets." Many are in languages other than English.

COURAGE TO CHANGE: Catalog For Life's Challenges
Order: 1-800-440-4003 (free catalogue)

> Mail order catalogue with items such as T shirts, mugs, writing material, books, pamphlets, etc. There is a "Loss and Grief" section with books for both adults and children. Prices range, in this section, from $10.00 to $24.00. Nice touch: owners state they do not sell their mailing list.

"Estate Planning Through Trusts"
Neuberger & Berman Trust Co.
605 3rd Ave. New York, NY 10158

> A free booklet that explains types of trusts and the pitfalls of not setting them up properly.

"FACTS for consumers — Funerals: A Consumer Guide" from the Federal Trade Commission, Office of Consumer/Business Education
FTC Headquarters, 6th & Pennsylvania Ave. N.W., Washington, DC 20580
Atten: Public Reference
Phone: 202-326-3650 (English)
Phone: 202-326-2222 (Spanish)

> Handy four-pager with funeral industry practices [rules] and a list of places one may contact for more information and complaints. Addressees and phone numbers tend to be out-of-date. (Free)

"Personal Thoughts About Medical Treatment and Related Values and Views Workbook" by Healthcare and Elder Law Programs Corporation, 1997. $5.00. Order: 1-310-540-2601 (Los Angeles area, CA) or see Web listing.

> HELP is a community-funded, non-profit information resources for Older Adults. The workbook is not a legal document but a help in articulating wishes and help with the communication between legal, medical and others. Easy to read, understand and do the written exercises.

"The Bereaved Child: The Road To Recovery" by Dr. Glen W. Davidson, 1992. OGR Service Corporation, P.O. Box 3586, Springfield, IL, 62708.

> Clear, concise and available at funeral homes.

Certain religions and ethnic traditions dictate avoidance of corpses. Some individuals feel fearful or avoid the face of death. Others may want to stay, touch or even get into bed and hold the deceased as a way of grieving and saying good-bye. Buddhists, as an example, will sit with the deceased, burn incense, and do a ceremony.

Organizations/Businesses

No attempt has been made to literally list all organizations connected with death and dying. Listed here are organizations that provided information for this book and would be helpful for the reader. For example, a reader may find the idea of "cryonics" to be interesting and would like to get more information about this and will find the "International Cryonics Foundation" organization listed. This is not the only source of information on cryonics but it would be a start.

Alzheimer's Association, National Headquarters (Chicago)
Phone: 1-800-272-3900

> The national headquarters will provide printed
> material and local referrals.

Alzheimer's Association, Honolulu Chapter, Inc.
1050 Ala Moana Blvd. Bldg. D
Honolulu, Hawai'i 96813-4906
Phone: 808-591-1771
FAX: 808-595-0570

> The Honolulu chapter sells "Dammit Dolls", a stuffed
> doll about 12 inches in height, $7.00. A cute gift for
> either caregiver or patient. A good stress reliever. The
> creation did not originate in Honolulu, other chapters
> may have.

American Association of Retired Persons
AARP Fulfillment
601 E. Street, N.W., Washington, D.C. 20049
WEB www.aarp.org

> AARP is a nonprofit, nonpartisan organization dedicated
> to helping older (50+) Americans. Publishes "Funeral
> Goods and Services" and "Pre-Paying for Your Funeral".
> (Free)

American Academy of Psychiatry
(Committee on Geriatric Psychiatry and the Law)
Phone: 1-800-331-1389

> Geriatric psychiatrists specialize in mental
> problems of the elderly as they relate to legal
> matters. The AAP can provide referrals for your
> area. The AAP recommends when legalities are
> concerned, the person's attorney should request the
> services of a forensic psychiatrist — a physician who
> specializes in assessing behavior for legal purposes.

American Bar Association
541 North Fairbanks Court
Chicago, Illinois 60611-3314
Phone: 1-800-285-2221

> This is the national legal organization and is not affili-
> ated with the state Bar Associations. However, they can
> let you know if your state has a state Bar Association. If
> it does they can give you a name and phone number.
> They also have (for a fee) a nation-wide directory they
> can send to you.

American Board of Funeral Service Education
14 Crestwood Road
Cumberland, Maine 04021
Phone: 207-829-5715
FAX: 207-829-4443

> An accreditation board for colleges and programs of
> funeral service and mortuary science.

Celestis, Inc
2444 Times Blvd. Ste 260
Houston, TX 77005
Phone: 1-800-522-3217
WEB: www.celestis.com
E-mail <Celestis@iah.com>

> For-profit business dealing in commemorative
> cremain scattering in outer space.

Center For Thanatology and Education Inc.
391 Atlantic Ave.
Brooklyn, NY 11217
Phone: 718-858-3026   FAX: same number
WEB: thanatolgy.org
E-mail <rhalporn@pipeline.com>

> One needs to call in advance to visit this book store,
> resource library and small press relating to death,
> dying, bereavement and gravestone studies. The propri-
> etor, Roberta, is available for lectures and
> presentations on thanatolgy and/or gravestone
> studies. Free catalogue upon request. Excellent resource
> location and person.

Children of Aging Parents
(Levittown, PA)
Phone: 1-800-227-7294

> National headquarters. Support groups throughout the
> US for adults who are or will be caregivers of their
> aging parents. Call for nearest location to you.
> NOTE: Los Angeles is not affiliated with the
> national organization. For help in the L.A. area call
> 310-476-9777, ext. 215.

Cremation Association of North America
401 North Michigan Avenue
Chicago, Illinois 60611
Phone: 312-644-6610

> CANA is an association of crematories, cemeteries, and funeral homes that offer cremation with over 1,100 screened members. Referrals and free brochures are available. Funded by membership dues.

Courage To Change
(Book Catalog)
P.O. Box 2140
Craneberry Twp, PA 16066
Phone: 1-800-440-4003

> Call the 800 number for a free catalog which includes a section on "Loss and Grief" with books for both adults and children.

Eldercare Locator
Phone: 1-800-677-1116
(Wash DC)

> A public service funded through the US Administration on Aging which provides names and addresses of eldercare related offices/organizations/ departments in your area.

Funeral Consumers Alliance
P.O. Box 10
Hinesburg, VT 05461
WEB: www.funerals.org
Phone: 802-482-3437

> A non-profit organization that disseminates information about planning and funeral costs with local autonomous affiliates throughout the US. Call for nearest affiliate. Excellent, informative online Web site.

Funeral Service Consumer Assistance Program
National Research and Information Center
1614 Central Street
Evanston, Illinois 60201
Phone: 1-800-662-7666

> Arbitrates consumer complaints concerning funeral related purchases.

HEIRS®: An Organization of Beneficiaries For Trust/Estate Reform
Standish H. Smith, Founder & President
P.O. Box 292
Villanova, PA 19085
Phone: 610-527-6260
WEB: www.heirs.net

> A non-profit dues paying membership organization dedicated to the reform of trust/estate administration. HEIRS® offers advice, printed material and political expertise to both people wanting to create a trust and beneficiaries of trusts.

The Hemlock Society USA
P.O. Box 101810
Denver, Colorado 80250
Phone: 1-800-247-7421

> National membership society with most states, but not all, having local societies. Education, legislative lobbying and literature dealing with euthanasia-assisted suicide issues.

International Association for Medical Assistance to Travelers
417 Center Street
Lewiston, NY 14092
Phone: 716-754-4883

IMAT will send a free membership card (donations welcome), a world directory of doctors, a fee schedule agreed to be charged by these doctors, immunization charts, etc.

International Cryonics Foundation
1430 No. El Dorado
Stockton, California
Phone: 209-463-0429

A non-profit organization that can provide literature, names and addresses of other cryonic organizations, help with filling out a cryonic application. The public is invited to their bi-annual meetings with the board of directors.

Islamic Center of Southern California
434 So. Vermont Ave.
Los Angeles, CA, 90020
Phone: 213-382-9200

A Muslim mosque in central Los Angeles, the tiny staff is friendly and will try to answer questions and provide phone number/address of other American mosques.

Jewish Funeral Directors of America, Inc.
Seaport Landing,
150 Lynnway
Suite 506
Lynn, Mass 01901
Phone: 212-628-3465

JFDA is a national trade association of funeral directors serving the Jewish community. It has approximately 250 members.

Monument Builders of North America
3158 S. River Road, Suite 224
Des Plaines, IL 60018
Phone: 847-803-8800

A membership trade organization of 900 independent monument builders. May contact them for the brochure "Buying A Monument", a general information guide. There are 4,500 independent builders in the US and MBNA is not a consumer complaints or arbitration organization.

National Academy of Elder Law Attorneys
1604 North Country Club
Tucson, AZ 85716
Phone: 520-881-4005

The public may call for assistance in obtaining brochures on elder-law related issues, such as finding an elder-law attorney, medicare, medicaid, etc. Fee and free.

National Association of Crime Victim Compensation Boards
P.O. Box 16003
Alexandria, Virginia
Phone: 703-370-2996

A government funded national headquarters. Provides referrals for local offices in all 50 states. Financial compensation for those who have been attacked and those who have suffered because a family member was injured or killed. Money is available to those who have already tapped insurance and other available sources for help.

National Association of Geriatric Care Managers
1604 North Country Club Road
Tucson, AZ 85716
Phone: 520-881-8008

Able to get referrals of geriatric care managers in your area. Call or send in a stamped self-addressed envelope.

National Domestic Violence Hotline
Phone: 1-800-799-SAFE
TDD: 1-800-787-3224

National Funeral Directors Association
11121 West Oklahoma Avenue
Milwaukee, Wisconsin 53227
Phone: 414-541-2500

NFDA is the largest educational and professional association of funeral directors. Established in 1882, it has 14,000 members throughout the US.

National Funeral Directors and Morticians Association
3951 Snapfinger Parkway
Suite 570
Decatur, GA 30035
Phone: 404-286-6680

NFDMA is a national association primarily of black funeral providers. It has 2,000 members. Provides regulatory guidelines and a national network of funeral providers. "National Scope" quarterly magazine devoted to multi-cultural issues with a focus on the African-American, both cultural and funeral provider trends. Provides educational (open forums) information.

National Hospice Organization
1901 North Moore Street , Suite 901
Arlington, Virginia 22209
Phone: 703-243-5900
Hospice Helpline: 1-800-658-8898
NHO Bookstore: 1-800-646-6460
Children's Hospice International: 1-800-24-CHILD
Medicare Hospice Hotline: 1-800-638-8633

National Prison Hospice Association
Phone: 303-443-8633

>A non-profit advocacy for providers and consumers.
Can help with referrals, information, problems, etc.

National Selected Morticians, Inc.
5 Revere Dr., Ste 340
Northbrook, Illinois, 60062
Phone: 1-800-323-4219

>An independent trade association of privately owned
funeral homes both in the U.S. and foreign countries.
Will provide information to the public on international
repatriation (out-of-country return), mortuary schools
and pre-planning.

(1) Parents of Murdered Children &
Other Survivors of Homicide
100 East 8th Street B-41
Cincinnati, Ohio 45202
Phone: 513-721-5683

>The national headquarters with referrals to 300 chap-
ters and contact people. Services provided include
printed material with self-help programs and telephone
support. Founded in 1978 by parents of a murdered

child who wanted to talk about their murdered child but friends and family could not.

(2) Compassionate Friends
P.W. Box 3696
Oak Brook, IL 60533-3696
Phone: 877-969-0010
www.compassionatefriends.org

This organization gives support to parents whose children have died.

Recovery Inc. (headquarters)
802 N. Dearborn Street
Chicago, IL 60610
Phone: 312-337-5661

A non-profit organization for self-help training for people unable to cope with situations in their lives. Local Recovery Inc located throughout the US. Check your local phone book or send a self-addressed stamped envelope to the address above.

Resources for the Family Funeral
P.O. Box 1720
Kamuela, Hawaii 96743
Phone/FAX: 808-775-9940
E-mail: dovetail@ilhawaii.net

An organization that provides information and materials needed to create a sort of "do-it-yourself" family funeral. Short but good resource listing, The Family Funeral is a concise informative book. Book cost: $9.95. Friendly people.

Summum
707 Genesee Ave.
Salt Lake, Utah 84104
Phone: 801-355-0137
www.Summum.org

> A non-profit organization that provides
> mummification for those who wish. Call for
> free brochure.

Viatical Association of America
Phone: 1-800-842-9811
WEB: www.cais.net/viatical

> Those who are terminally ill and need cash can find
> out more about viatical settlements by calling (or the
> internet) the VAA, which offers a free booklet that
> explains more about the industry and how to obtain
> such a settlement.

Author's Bibliography

People and Organizations

Mahmoud Abdel-Baset, Islamic Center of Southern California, Los Angeles, California.

Arthur Akeley, CWO, U.S. Coast Guard, Decedent Affairs Officer, Honolulu, Hawaii.

Jim Allen, Captain/Paramedic, Clinton Fire and Rescue, Clinton, Mississippi. President, National Association of Emergency Medical Technicians.

Theodore J. "Ted" Aquaro, Secretary-Treasurer, Los Angeles Firemen's Relief Association, Inc., Los Angeles, California.

Father John Bakas, Dean of St. Sophia Greek Orthodox Cathedral, Los Angeles, California.

Brad Bates, Disposition Branch, Air Force Mortuary Affairs, San Antonio, Texas.

John Blake, Executive Director & Betty Blake, Secretary, (RET) Funeral and Memorial Societies of America, Inc., Egg Harbor, Wisconsin.

Dr. Charles Brown, Staff Minister, Understanding Principles For Better Living Church, Los Angles, California.

Susan Buckley, National Hospice Organization, Arlington, Virginia.

Lisa Carlson, Exe. Dir. Funeral and Memorial Societies of America, Inc., Hinesburg, Vermont.

Scott Carrier, Spokesman, Department of Coroner, Los Angeles County, California.

Mrs. Dorothy Conley, Parish Secretary, Saint Timothy's Catholic Church, Los Angeles, California.

Debbie Everitt, Cruise Consultant, Cruise Specialists, Marina del Rey, California.

Terence Francis, Fire Marshal, Burlington, Vermont.

WN2 Debbie Gordon, Yeoman, 2nd Class, Coast Guard, Honolulu, Hawaii.

HNC L. Gorham, USN, Leading Chief Petty Officer, US Navy Mortuary Affairs, Great Lakes, Illinois.

Alfonso Hidalgo, Mortician, Armstrong Family Malloy-Mitten, Los Angeles, California.

Rabbi Israel Hirsch, Los Angeles, California.

Paul Hultquist, Director, Learning Resource Center, The Valley Funeral Home, Inc., Burbank, California.

Phil Hunt, Funeral Director, The Valley Funeral Home, Burbank, California.

Barbara Jones, Program Analyst, Policy and Procedure Section, California Board of Control, Sacramento, California.

Barbara Joseph, RN, MA, Registered Nurse & Psychotherapy Intern, Los Angeles, California.

Angelo Karamanis, MA, Psychology, Los Angeles, California.

Daniel P. Kapahu, Funeral Director, Hosoi Garden Mortuary, Honolulu, Hawaii.

Michael Kubasak, President, Valley Funeral Home, Inc., Burbank, California.

Officer Jason Lee, Public Information Officer, Los Angeles Police Department, Los Angeles, California.

Leon Leonard, The Neptune Society, San Pedro, California.

Dr. Calvin Lum, Veterinarian, Department of Agriculture, Honolulu, Hawaii.

Gwendolyn Moore, Licensed Clinical Social Worker, Licensed Mortician, Atlanta, Georgia.

Betty Murray, National Foundation of Funeral Service, Des Plaines, Illinois.

Stephen Naramore , Public Relations, Princess Cruises. Los Angeles, California.

Barbara Nelson, Administrative Director, Cremation Association of North America, Chicago, Illinois.

HMC Gene Paul, Navy Liaison Unit, Honolulu, Hawaii.

David Perry, Funeral Director, Robert Pumphrey Funeral Homes, Bethesda, Maryland.

Craig Peterson, PsyD , Pasadena, California.

Art Quife, Ph.D., President, Trans Time, Inc., Oakland, California.

Corky Ra, Founder, Summum, Salt Lake City, Utah.

Jihane Rohrbacker, Communications Director, NAPGCM & NAELA, Tucson, Arizona.

Prithvi Raj Singh, President, Southern California Federation of Hindu Associations, California.

Les Stewart (US Army, RET), Contracting Officer Representative, Hawaii.

Marge Strand, Executive Secretary, Los Angeles Funeral Society, California.

Andrew L. Synder, BA, LFD, Executive Assistant, National Selected Morticians, Inc., Northbrook, Illinois.

Dr. Bob Swacker, New York University, New York, New York.

Jacquie Taylor, President, San Francisco College of Mortuary Science, San Francisco, California.

Tracy Taylor, Librarian, Los Angeles Public Library, Los Angeles, California.

Hank Turk, Dir. of Public Safety, Pascogoula , Mississippi

Atrgovind Vyas, Pujari (Hindu temple priest), Hawaiian Gardens, California.

Kathleen Walczak, Research & Information, National Funeral Directors Association, Milwaukee, Wisconsin.

Michael H. White, Lawyer, Santa Monica, Califiornia.

Ralph Williams (CDR USN RET), Retired Affairs (Navy), Pearl Harbor, Hawaii.

Leo Zavala, General Insurance Agent, Los Angeles, California.

Jack Zin, President, International Cryonics Foundation, Stockton, California.

Print

BOOKS

Death And Dignity: Making Choices and Taking Charge, 1993,
    Timothy E. Quill, MD, W.W. Norton & Co.: New York.

Death to Dust: What Happens to Dead Bodies, 1994,
    Kenneth V. Iserson, M.D., Galen Press, Ltd., Arizona.

Death and Dying: Views from Many Cultures, 1980,
    Richard A. Kalish (Editor Baywood Publishing Company,
    Inc.: New York.

Death: The Final Stage of Growth, 1975, Elisabeth Kübler-Ross
    (Editor), Prentice-Hall, Inc.: New Jersey. Chapters include:
    "Dying Among Alaskan Indians: A Matter of Choice,"
    Murray L. Trelease
    "The Jewish View of Death: Guidelines For Dying,"
    Zachary I. Heller
    "The Jewish View of Death: Guidelines For Mourning,"
    Audrey Gordon
    "The Death That Ends Death in Hinduism and Buddhism,"
    J. Bruce Long.

Embalming: History, Theory, and Practice, 1990, Robert G. Mayer,
    Appleton & Lange: Connecticut.

Ethnic Variations in Dying, Death, and Grief: Diversity in Universality,
1993, Donald P. Irish, Kathleen F. Lundquist &
    Vivian Jenkins Nelsen (Editors), Taylor & Francis:
    Washington D.C.

The Family Funeral, 1995, Julie Wiskind & Richard Spiegel,
    Dovetail: Hawaii.

Funeral Customs The World Over, 1974, Robert W. Habenstein &
   William M. Lamers, Bulfin Printers, Inc.: Milwaukee.

Grief Counseling & Grief Therapy, 1991, (Second Edition)
   J. William Worden, Springer Publishing Company: New York.

The History of American Funeral Directing, 1962, (Revised
   Edition) Robert W. Habenstein & William H. Lamers, Bulfin
   Printers, Inc.: Wisconsin.

*How to Be a Perfect Stranger: A Guide to Etiquette in Other People's
Religious Ceremonies*, 1996, Arthur J. Magida (Editor),
   Jewish Lights Publishing: Vermont.

The Jewish Way in Death and Mourning, 1969, Maurice Lamm,
   Jonathan David Publishers: New York.

Learning To Say Goodbye: When A Parent Dies, 1976,
   Eda LeShan, Macmillan Publishing Co., Inc.: New York.

Someone You Love Is Dying: A Guide For Helping and Coping,
   1975, Martin Shepard, M.D., Harmony Books: New York.

The Hour Of Our Death, 1981, Philippe Ariès, Alfred A. Knopf,
   Inc.: New York. L'Homme devant la mort, 1977, Éditions du
   Seuil: Paris.

The Nuts and Bolts of Surviving the Loss or Illness of a Loved One,
1990, Barbara T. Cochrane, BS & Helen F. McGrane, PhD,
   Regenesis Publishing: California.

They Need To Know, 1979, Audrey K. Gordon & Dennis Klass,
   Prentice-Hall: New Jersey.

When A Child Dies: Ways You Can Help A Bereaved Parent, 1995,
   Bonnie Hunt Conrad, Fithian Press: California.

Widow, 1974, Lynn Caine, Morrow: New York.

Articles

"Catholic Funeral Ritual Emphasizes Burial Service," The Rev. Terence P. Curley, D.Min, <u>American Funeral Director Magazine</u>, February, 1992.

"Serving the Mormon Community," Scott S. Smith, <u>American Funeral Director Magazine</u>, April, 1992.

"The Language Challenge," Scott S. Smith, and "The Traditional Jewish Funeral", Gere Caputo, <u>American Funeral Director Magazine</u>, October, 1992.

"Burial practices and attitudes toward death: Cultural differences," Linda Sue King, <u>Thanatos,</u> Fall,1982, (Vol. 7, No. 3).

"Cremation...are you at risk?," Michael Kubasak, <u>Traditions</u>, Fall, 1995, (Vol. 1, No. 3).

"Special Preneed Comparison Issue," Alan Severson, Editor, <u>Funeral Monitor</u>, August 14, 1995, (Vol. 4, No. 31).

IN-HOUSE ARTICLES

"Contemporary Cremation Practices: A Guide For The Consumer," Mike Kubasak, Valley Funeral Home, Inc., Burbank, California.

"How To Be There In The Last Hours Of Life With A Loved One", AIDS PROJECT Los Angeles, California.

Index

I Would Love to Hear Your Story

IF YOU HAVE A STORY that would help others who will need to handle the details before or after someone's death, I invite you to send them to me. If appropriate, I will share them either in future editions of my book or on my website—with your permission, of course.

Don't worry about the form or how well or badly you think you write. Just send in your experience and we will clean it up if required. It's a great opportunity for us to reach out and help others during their tough time.

Send your stories to:

Judith Lee
9854 National Blvd. Ste. 109
Los Angeles, CA 90034

Email: **judy@judithlee.com**

Thanks.

Judith Lee

How to Engage the Author

AS MUCH AS WE MIGHT PREFER it otherwise, dealing with the after-effects of the death of a friend or loved one is inevitable. However, you can make it much easier by being prepared.

Judith Lee delivers talks on how to anticipate what will be necessary, covering all the bases, dotting the i's and crossing the t's. She treats this serious subject with respect tempered with a lightness that leaves audiences smiling with the confidence of knowing they will know what to do if they need to act on someone's behalf.

Judy is also available for consultation by phone for those with terminally ill loved ones or those who simply want to know in advance what their choices may be and how to make the best ones—for everyone involved.

Email: judy@judithlee.com

www.JudithLee.com

www.JudithLee.com